THE SLIDE RULE

FOR

SEA AND AIR NAVIGATION

THE SLIDE RULE

FOR

SEA AND AIR NAVIGATION

An introduction to the slide rule, with special reference to Navigation, both at sea and in the air, and problems encountered in cargo working and other ship and aircraft handling

BY

J. C. PODMORE

GLASGOW
BROWN, SON & FERGUSON, LIMITED
52 DARNLEY STREET

First Edition - 1933
Second Edition - 1957
Third Edition - 1974

© 1974 Brown, Son & Ferguson, Ltd., Glasgow, G41 2SG.
Printed and Made in Geeat Britain.

INTRODUCTION.

IT is remarkable how few seamen and airmen realise the simplicity and speed of a slide rule.

Many problems involving long calculations, normally worked either by logarithms or long methods of arithmetic, can be worked on the slide rule in a matter of seconds.

It would seem that there is an impression that a slide rule is difficult to manipulate, takes a long time to master, and that constant practice is required for proficiency.

On the contrary, learning to use a slide rule is like learning to ride a bicycle; simple to learn, does not take long, and once learnt is never forgotten.

This book is intended to show how to use a slide rule with understanding, for the solution of the many problems in Navigation, Flight planning, Cargo work, and other everyday calculations met with by Seamen and Airmen.

CONTENTS

CHAPTER IX—MISCELLANEOUS PROBLEMS

Compass problems—Gyro calculations—Angle of deflection—
Revolutions, pitch and speed—Fuel consumption   109

CONTENTS.

CONTENTS

CHAPTER IX—MISCELLANEOUS PROBLEMS

APPENDIX

The Slide Rule
For Sea and Air Navigation

CHAPTER I

CHOICE OF RULE

To obtain the best results from the slide rule, the rule must be suitable for the uses to which it will be put. There are a great number of different rules on the market, each designed with some particular object in view. There are at least three rules which have been designed for Navigators.

Obviously, the rule required must be one on which ordinary numerical calculations, and also those involving trigonometrical ratios, can be worked in the simplest manner. In many rules the ordinary calculating scales are found on one side of the slide and the trigonometrical ratios on the other side. With this type of rule, either the slide has to be reversed in the middle of some calculations, or the ratios have to be read off the back of the slide and then set on the rule.

On other types, all the scales, both numerical and trigonometrical are given on the one face. This makes for simplicity of making calculations, though at first sight the rule may appear complicated, owing to the number of scales. However, this type of rule has many advantages, and, once understood, is far easier to use than the other type.

For this reason the rule selected and used in all these calculations in this book is of the latter type. The Academy Duplex 504, made by Blundell-Harling Ltd. This is a double-sided rule, having scales on both the front and back of the rule and slide.

A further advantage of this rule is the inclusion of a scale of Tangents of Angles over 45°. This scale is seldom found on other rules, but is of real advantage for any problem involving Tangents.

When choosing the rule look to see that the graduations are clear and sharp, that the slide moves freely and does not stick, but is not too free. Set the Cursor to the index of the D scale, and see that it lies directly over the index of the A scale; then set it to any number on the D scale and see that it cuts the A scale at the square of that number.

A cheap rule is seldom a good investment. In time the scales may warp, as also may the rule itself, and the slide often either starts to stick or else run too freely. Many a beginner has been put off by trying to use such a rule.

Description of the Rule.

The rule described is the 'Academy Duplex 504, mentioned in the 'Choice of rule'.

The Rule consists of three parts:
1. The Stock, or Rule itself.
2. The Slide.
3. The Cursor.

Both the stock and slide carry scales, each lettered to identify them. For ease in making calculations all the trigonometrical scales are on the face of the rule and can be used in conjunction with each other.

Considering first the Face of the Rule.

On the upper edge of the rule are certain gauge points.

THE TRIGONOMETRICAL SCALES

Scales TA and TB.

These scales are scales of Tangents. The TA scale reading from 5° 45′ to 45° and the TB scale from 45° to 84° 15′.

On the TA scale every 5′ is marked up to 20° and from 20° to 45° every 10′.

On the TB scale every 10′ of arc is marked over the whole range of the scale.

The ST Scale.

This is a scale of Sines and Tangents of small angles up to 5° 45′. For angles in this range the sine and tangent may be considered equal, with no appreciable loss of accuracy. This scale then, is used for either.

The scale is marked for every ½′ (30″) up to 1°, then every 1′ of arc up to 5°, and above 5° for every 5′ of arc.

The S Scale.

This is used for both Sines and Cosines. The sine scale reading from left to right from 5° 45′ to 90°, is graduated for every 5′ up to 10°, every 10′ from 10° to 20°, every 20′ from 20° to 40°, every 30′ from 40° to 70°, every 1° from 70° to 80°, and every 2° from 80° to 90°.

The same graduations are used for the cosine scales, the figures for which read from right to left from 0° at the right index to 84° 15′ at the left index of the scale.

The SI Scale.

This scale of Sines on the rule, reads from 0° to 90°, from left to right, and, in brackets, from 90° to 180°, reading from right to left. The graduations are similar to those on the S scale, but since this scale really comprises both the ST and S scales on the length of one of them, it is not so closely graduated.

The K Scale.

This scale of Cubes consists of three scales placed end to end, each similar to the C and D scales, but naturally less closely graduated.

The L Scale.

This is a scale of Inches, reading to 1/50 of an inch, and is used, with the other scales, to find the mantissa of the logarithms of numbers.

Other types of Slide Rule.

The 'Academy Duplex 504', used for all the settings in this book, has the C and D, A and B, and all Trigonometrical Scales engraved on the face of the rule. Many rules, even some designed as navigational rules, do not have as convenient a lay-out of the scales. In such rules the Sine and Tangent scales are frequently to be found on the reverse of the slide. This arrangement of scales has the disadvantage that the slide has to be reversed in order to use these ratios. When this occurs in the middle of a calculation, it results in delay and a possible loss of accuracy.

To reverse the slide, withdraw it completely, turn it over and reinsert it in the rule, when the Sine and Tangent scales appear on the face. It may then be used exactly as described in the text of this book.

For example—To solve:

$$\frac{30}{50} \sin 48°.$$

Set 50 on C over 30 on D, move the cursor to the index of C, reverse the slide, set the index of S to the cursor, move the cursor to 48° on S and read 0·445 on D.

On very few rules is the second scale of tangents, TB included. This is a scale of the Tangents of Angles over 45°. This scale is not strictly an essential, but saves much extra calculation.

When the tangent of an angle over 45° is required, on a rule which does not include the TB scale, it has to be remembered that $\tan \theta = \dfrac{1}{\tan (90 - \theta)}$ and therefore that to multiply by $\tan \theta$ one can divide by $\tan (90 - \theta)$ and vice versa. This frequently leads to confusion. It is strongly recommended that any formula containing the tangent of an angle over 45°, be rewritten before putting on the rule.

Thus $\sin 30 . \cot 52 = \sin 30 . \tan 38 \ (90 - 52)$
or

$$\frac{\cos 50}{\cot 63} = \frac{\cos 50}{\tan 27}$$

It will also be found that most rules have only a scale of sines and that cosines are not marked. This is simply overcome by remembering that $\cos \theta = \sin (90 - \theta)$.

That is to say that where the cosine of an angle is required, use the sine of its complement.

A further important difference, frequently found on slide rules, is that there is no ST scale, for the sines and tangents of small angles but that the sine scale reads from 0° 35′ to 90°, and the tangent scale from 5° 45′ to 45°.

In this case the sine scale is used for the tangents of all angles less than 5° 45′.

On this type of rule the sine scale must be used with the A and B scales, and the tangent scale with the C and D scales. That is to say that calculations involving both sines and tangents cannot be made directly.

For example—Error in Longitude for an error of 1′ in Latitude.

Error = cot az. sec. Lat.

Given. Azimuth 070°, Lat. 37° 30′
Error = cot 70. sec 37° 30′

This must be rewritten as:

$$\text{Error} = \frac{\tan 20°}{\cos 37° 30′} = \frac{\tan 20}{\sin 52° 30′}$$

First centre the slide and set the cursor to 20° on the tan scale and read 0·364 on D.

Then set the cursor to ·364 on A and set 52° 30′ on the sine scale to the cursor. Then over the index of the sine scale read 0·458 on A.

Alternatively—$\tan \theta = \dfrac{\sin \theta}{\cos \theta}$

$$\therefore \frac{\tan 20°}{\sin 52° 30′} = \frac{\sin 20°}{\cos 20° \times \sin 52° 30′} = \frac{\sin 20°}{\sin 70° \times \sin 52° 30′}$$

Now set 70 on the sine scale to the index of A, move the cursor to 20 on the sine scale, set 52° 30′ on the sine scale to the cursor and over the index of the slide read ·458 on A.

It is on account of these inconveniences, in this type of rule, that the 'Navigators Slide Rule', with all scales on the one face, and all constructed to the same scale, has been selected and recommended.

THE PRINCIPLE OF THE SLIDE RULE

Before making use of any instrument it is advisable to have some understanding of the principle on which it works. This gives an appreciation of its possibilities, capabilities and limitations.

The principle used in the slide rule is a simple technique of adding or subtracting numbers by means of two similar rulers.

The figure shows two rulers, A and B, of equal length, each divided into 10 equal parts. The upper, or A rule, being fixed, and the lower, or B rule, capable of sliding either way.

Any such pair of rules may be used to add or subtract numbers mechanically.

If the zero on the B rule is set to the 4 on the A rule, then over any number on B will be found 4 plus that number, on the A.

For instance, over 3 on B is found 7 on A. The total length, from 0 on A to 7 on B, is 4 on A plus 3 on B. Since the scales are identical this gives 3 plus 4 = 7.

For subtraction, if 5 on B is set to 9 on A, then over 0 on B is found 9−5, or 4 on A. In this case the length of 5 units of the B has been deducted from 9 units of the A.

Suppose that it is required to find 4+8 by means of the two rules. The 8 on the B rule lies beyond the end of the A rule. That is beyond 10. Therefore the sum of 4 and 8 is more than 10. If the A rule were not fixed, this rule could be moved up so that the 0 on the A cuts the B rule, where the 10 is at present, i.e. at 6 on the B rule. Then over 8 on the B read 2 on A. Since the number, as has been shewn, is more than 10, this would be 10+2, or 12.

B

However, it is the B that can be moved. The same result can be obtained by setting the 10 on the B, to the present position of the O on B, i.e. at 4 on A. That is to say, slide the B rule its complete length to the left, when over 8 on B will be found 2 on A.

The slide rule uses the same technique, but with this difference: the graduations on the rules are not of equal length, but in proportion to the logarithms of the numbers. Therefore, instead of adding or subtracting numbers, the slide rule adds or subtracts logarithms.

Adding and subtracting the logarithms of numbers is equivalent to multiplication and division.

Consider the C, D and L scales on the face of the rule.

The L scale is a scale of inches, and all the scales are 10 inches in length.

Set the cursor to 2 on the D scale and it will cut the L scale at ·301, or 3·01 inches. Therefore the length of the D scale, from the index to 2, is 3·01 inches, or ·301 of the total length of the scale. But, $Log_{10}2 = 0·301$.

Similarly, set the cursor to 3 on D and it will cut the L scale at ·477. $Log_{10}3 = ·477$.

Again, set the cursor to 6 on D and it will cut the L scale at ·778. $Log_{10}6 = ·778$.

Now set the index of the C scale to 2 on the D scale, and move the cursor to 3 on the C scale. The cursor cuts the D scale at 6 and the L scale at ·778.

From the index of D to 2 is   3·01″ $Log_{10}2 = ·301$

From the index of C to 3 is   4·77″ $Log_{10}3 = ·477$

From the index of D to 3 on C 7·78″ $Log_{10}6 = ·778$

The slide rule has automatically added $\log_{10}2$ to $\log_{10}3$, and shewn the product of 2×3 as 6, on the D scale.

Similarly, if the 3 on the C scale is set over 6 on the D scale, under the index of the C scale will be found 2; the number whose $\log_{10}$ is $\log_{10}6 - \log_{10}3$. That is to say $6 \div 3 = 2$.

The slide rule, therefore, provides a quick and simple means of multiplying and dividing, using a mechanical method of adding and subtracting logarithms.

It must be remembered that a logarithm has two parts, a characteristic and a mantissa. The slide rule provides the mantissa. That is to say that any number on the rule may represent that number multiplied or divided by any multiple of 10. For example 3, 0·3, 0·003, 30, 30,000, etc., are represented by the same mark on the rule. The characteristic is found by inspection, or by using very simple rules which will be explained later.

MULTIPLE HAIRLINE CURSORS

On some rules the cursor will be found to have more than one hairline. The purpose of the extra hairlines is to assist in certain calculations.

Set the left-hand line to the index of C and the right hand one will be found to cut the C scale at 'C'. These lines will be found, therefore, to be of use in problems involving the area of a circle.

For example—To find the volume of a cylinder whose length is 14 feet and diameter 3 feet.

Set the index of C to 3 on D, set the right-hand hairline of the cursor to 14 on B, and under the left-hand line read 99 on A.

Volume—99 cu. ft.

Example—Required the area of a circle of diameter 8 feet.

Set the right-hand line to 8 on D, and read 50·1 under the left-hand line on A.

Area—50·1 sq. ft.

See page 44 for an explanation of this setting.

CHAPTER II

MULTIPLICATION, DIVISION, SQUARE ROOTS CUBE ROOTS, AND LOGARITHMS

General.

1. Whenever the cursor is mentioned, it is the hairline engraved on it that is indicated.

2. Always use the cursor for making settings and reading results; this ensures greater accuracy.

3. When the index of a scale is referred to, either index may be used, as appropriate.

4. Centre the slide, means set the index of the slide coincident with the index of the rule.

5. To set a number on the slide to a given number on the rule, set the cursor to the given number on the rule, then draw out the slide till the required number on the slide lies under the cursor.

6. Should the required graduation on the slide lie outside the limit of the rule, set the cursor to the index of the slide and set the other index of the slide to the cursor, when the graduation required will be found to lie within the limits of the rule.

7. When it is required to read on one scale under or over a number on another scale, set the cursor to the given number and read off, on the requisite scale, under the cursor.

Multiplication.

As has previously been shown, multiplication is performed by adding lengths of the rule, the lengths being proportional to the logarithms of the numbers.

Rule.

Set the index of C over one of the factors on the D scale, move the cursor to the other factor on the C scale and where the cursor cuts the D scale, read the product.

Example—2×4.

Set the left index of C over 2 on D, move the cursor to 4 on C, and read 8 on D.

$$2 \times 4 = 8.$$

In this case the left index of C was used. If the right index of C had been placed over 2 on D, the 4 on C would lie outside the D scale.

Example—5×35.

Set the right index of C to 5 on D and under 35 on C read 175 on D.

$$5 \times 35 = 175.$$

In this case it has been necessary to use the right index to bring the 35 on C within the limits of the D scale.

Fixing the Position of the Decimal Point.

In most problems it will be obvious where the decimal point should be placed. But when necessary it may be found very simply, in much the same way as with logarithms.

As with logarithms use is made of the characteristic.

e.g.	Number	123478		Characteristic	+5.
	„	123·478		„	+2.
	„	1·23478		„	0.
	„	·00123478		„	−3.

That is to say that the characteristic is one less than the number of figures before the decimal, or one more than the number of noughts after the decimal. Positive for the former and negative for the latter.

Rule.

Take the sum of the characteristics of the numbers and to this, if the slide projects to the left, add one. The result is the characteristic of the product.

In the first of the above examples, the characteristic of 2 is 0, and that of 4 is 0.

Sum of characteristics $0+0 = 0$.

Since the slide projects to the right this is the characteristic of the product, which must then be 8.

In the second example, the sum of the characteristics is $0+1 = 1$. The slide projects to the left, add 1, characteristic of product is $1+1 = 2$. The product is, therefore, 175·0.

Multiplication of several numbers.

This will best be explained by an example.

Example—$0·27 \times 54 \times 380 \times 7$.

Set the index of C to ·27 on D and move the cursor to 54 on C, under the cursor on D is the product of ·27 and 54, so set the index of C to the cursor and move the cursor to 380 on C. Now under the cursor is ·27 $\times$ 54 $\times$ 380. Set the index of C to the cursor and move the cursor to 7 on C, now under the cursor, read ·27 $\times$ 54 $\times$ 380 $\times$ 7 on D, or 38700.

The rule for fixing the decimal point is similar to that already given.

To the sum of the characteristics of the numbers add one each time the slide projects to the left. The result is the characteristic of the product.

In this example:

Set the right index of C to 27 on D and move the cursor

to 54 on C, the slide projects to the left; now set the left index of C to the cursor and move the cursor to 38 on C, the slide projects to the right; next set the right index of C to the cursor and move the cursor to 7 on D, the slide projects to the left, and the cursor cuts the D scale at 387.

Sum of characteristics $= -1+1+2+0 = +2$
Slide projected to the left twice $\qquad +2$

$$\text{Sum} \quad +4$$

Characteristic of Product $+4$.

Answer: 38700.

Example—$\cdot0034 \times \cdot125 \times 4\cdot8 \times \cdot37500$.

Set the left index of C to 34 on D and move the cursor to 125 on C, the slide projects to the right, set the right index of C to the cursor and move the cursor to 48 on C, the slide projects to the left, now set the left index of C to the cursor and move the cursor to 375 on C, the slide projects to the right, and the cursor cuts the D scale at 765.

Sum of characteristics $= -3-1+0+4 = \quad 0$
Slide projected to the left once $\qquad +1$

Characteristic of product $\qquad = +1$

$$\therefore \text{ Product} = 76\cdot5.$$

Division.

This, as already explained, is performed by subtracting lengths of the rule.

Rule.

Set the cursor to the dividend on D, draw out the slide till the divisor, on C, lies under the cursor, then under the index of C read the quotient on D.

Example—7·2÷3.

Place the cursor to 7·2 on D, draw out the slide till 3 on C lies under the cursor and under the index of C read 2·4 on D.

                    Quotient = 2·4.

Example—18÷4·5.

Set 4·5 on C over 18 on D, then under the index of C read 4 on D.

                    Quotient = 4.

Fixing the Position of the Decimal Point.

The rule here is very similar to that in multiplication. Subtract the characteristic of the divisor from that of the dividend, and from this subtract one for each time the slide projects to the left.

In the first example:

> Difference of characteristics = 0−0 = 0
> Slide projects to the right   0
>
> Characteristic of quotient   0
>
> Quotient = 2·4.

In the second example:

> Difference of characteristics = 1−0 = −1
> Slide projects to the left   −1
>
> Characteristic of quotient   0
>
> Quotient = 4.

Example— $\dfrac{312}{5 \cdot 1 \times \cdot 003 \times 47}$

Set 51 on C over 312 on D, and move the cursor to the

index of C, the slide projects to the left; now set 3 on C to the cursor and move the cursor to the index of C, the slide projects to the right; now set 47 on C to the cursor and move the cursor to the index of C, the slide projects to the left, and the cursor cuts the D scale at 434.

$$\text{Characteristic of dividend} \quad = \quad 2$$
$$\text{Characteristic of divisor} = 0-3+1 = -2$$

$$\text{Difference} \quad = +4$$
$$\text{Slide projected to the left twice} \quad = -2$$

$$\text{Characteristic of quotient} \quad = +2$$

Quotient 434·0.

Combining Multiplication and Division.

The same rules apply here as for multiplication and division performed separately.

Again this will be best explained by a few examples.

To solve $\dfrac{36 \times 44}{19 \times 73}$

Set 19 on C over 36 on D, then under the index of C will be $36 \div 19$; this is division and the slide projects to the right, now move the cursor to 44 on C, this is multiplying $(36 \div 19)$ by 44, and the slide projects to the right. Next set 73 on C to the cursor, to divide by 73, the slide projects to the right, and under the index of C is 114 on D.

$$\text{Characteristic of dividend} = 1+1 = 2$$
$$\text{Characteristic of divisor} \quad = 1+1 = 2$$

$$\text{Difference} \quad = 0$$

The slide did not project to the left at any time, so the characteristic of the quotient is 0.

Answer: 1·14.

Example— $\dfrac{25 \times 18 \times 7}{13 \times 27}$

Set 13 on C over 25 on D. (division) slide projects to the right, move the cursor to 18 (multiplication) slide projects to the right, set 72 on C to the cursor (division) slide projects to the left, move the cursor to 7 on C (multiplication) slide projects to the left, and under the cursor read 336 on D.

Characteristic of dividend $1+1+0 =$	2
Characteristic of divisor $\quad 1+1 \quad =$	2
Difference $=$	0
Slide projected left once for mult.	$+1$
Slide projected left once for division	-1
Characteristic	0

Answer: 3·36.

Example— $\dfrac{35 \times 16 \times 32}{8 \times 64}$

Set 8 on C over 35 on D, (division) slide left, set the cursor to the right index of C and set the left index of C to the cursor, then move the cursor to 16 on C, (multiplication), slide right, set 64 on C to the cursor (division), slide right, move the cursor to 32 on C, (multiplication) slide right, and under the cursor read 35 on D.

Characteristic of dividend $1+1+1$ =   3
Characteristic of divisor $0+1$ =   1

Difference   2

Slide projected left once for division = -1

Characteristic of answer $+1$

Answer: 35.

Example— $$\frac{1\cdot1 \times 224 \times \cdot0024}{312 \times \cdot05 \times 57}$$

Set 312 on C over 1·1 on D (division) slide left, move the cursor to the index of C and set the left index of C to the cursor, then move the cursor to 224 on C (multiplication) slide right, set 5 on C to the cursor (division) slide right, move the cursor to 24 on C (multiplication) slide right, set 57 on C to the cursor (division) slide left, and under the index of C read 665 on D.

Characteristic of dividend $0+2-3$ = -1
Characteristic of divisor $2-2+1$ = $+1$

Difference   = -2

Slide projected left twice for division -2

Characteristic of answer -4

Answer: ·000665.

In the case of most calculations the approximate answer is already obvious. For instance, if finding the speed of a ship, the answer is '185', obviously it is 18·5 knots. The calculations here have been given in full to show how the position of the decimal point can be arrived at when a doubt does exist.

Any of the above examples could have been worked on the A and B scales instead of C and D, with some slight loss of accuracy, though the final positioning of the decimal would have been a far more complicated matter.

Use of the CF and DF Scales for Combined Multiplication and Division.

On the reverse of the rule are C/D and CF/DF scales. These can be used in conjunction with each other to avoid having to reset the slide when a number lies outside the limit of the D scale.

Example— $\dfrac{450 \times 114}{190}$

Set 190 on D to 450 on C, then over 114 on CF read 270 on DF.

Answer: 270.

Example— $\dfrac{14 \times 7}{9}$

Set 9 on CF to 14 on DF and over 7 on CF read 11·9 on DF.

Answer 10·9.

Squares and Square Roots of Numbers.

It has already been seen that the A and B scales are composed of two scales, each exactly half the length of the C and D scales. A little thought will show that if the cursor is set to any number on the D scale, it will cut the A scale at the number whose log is double that of the number on D. But to double the log is to square the number. Therefore, if the cursor is set to any number on D (or C) it will cut the A (or B) scale at the square of that number. And similarly, if the cursor is set to any number on the A (or B) scale it will cut the D (or C) scale at the square root of that number.

For example—Set the cursor to 3 on D and read 9 on A.
$$3^2 = 9$$

Set the cursor to 64 on A and read 8 on D
$$\sqrt[2]{64} = 8$$

To fix the Position of the Decimal Point.

In finding the square of a number. Set the cursor to the number on D, and note whether the square lies on the left or right scale of A.

Double the characteristic of the number and if it lies on the left scale of A this is the characteristic of the square, but if it lies on the right scale of A, add one to this.

For example—26^2.

Set the cursor to 26 on D and read 676 on A on the left-hand scale.

Characteristic of 26 is 1. $2 \times 1 = 2$

∴ characteristic of 26^2 is 2.

$$26^2 = 676$$

Example—$0 \cdot 07^2$.

Set the cursor to 7 on D and read 49 on the right-hand scale of A.

Characteristic is $(-2 \times 2) + 1 = -3$

$$\cdot 07^2 = \cdot 0049$$

Finding the Square Root.

If the characteristic of the number is even, halve it and set the cursor to the number on the left-hand scale of A, but if odd subtract one, then halve it and set the cursor to the number on the right-hand scale of A.

Example— $\sqrt[3]{7600}$

Characteristic of 7600 is 3.

∴ Use the right-hand scale of A and the characteristic will be $\dfrac{3-1}{2} = 1$.

Set the cursor to 76 on the right-hand scale of A and read 87·2 on D.

$$\sqrt[3]{7600} = 87·2$$

Example— $\sqrt[3]{·04}$.

Characteristic −2. Use left-hand of A and characteristic will be $\dfrac{-2}{2} = -1$.

Set the cursor to 4 on the left-hand scale of A and read ·2 on D.

$$\sqrt[3]{·04} = 0·2$$

Example— $\sqrt[3]{·0064}$.

Characteristic −3. Use right-hand scale of A and characteristic will be $\dfrac{-3-1}{2} = -2$.

Set the cursor to 64 on the right-hand scale of A and read ·08 on D.

$$\sqrt[3]{·0064} - 0·08$$

Problems involving squares and square roots can be worked very simply by using the A, B, C and D scales.

For example— 20×8^2.

Set the index of C to 8 on D and over 20 on B read 1280 on A.

$$20 \times 8^2 = 1280$$

When the index of C was set 8 on D, the index of B was automatically set to 8^2 (64) on A, by reading over 20 on B, the product of 64 and 20 is obtained.

Example—$(4 \times 15)^2$.

Set the index of C to 4 on D and move the cursor to 15 on C, then under the cursor is found 4×15 (60) on D, and the square of 60 (3600) on A.

$$(4 \times 15)^2 = 3600$$

Example— $\dfrac{7 \times 5^2}{18}$

Set the index of C to 5 on D, move the cursor to 7 on B, set 18 on B to the cursor and over the index of B read 9·72 on A.

Answer: 9·72.

Example— $\dfrac{9 \times 16}{7^2}$

Set the cursor to 9 on A, set 7 on C to the cursor, and over 16 on B read 2·95 on A.

Answer: 2·94.

Example—$1·2 \times \sqrt{42}$.

Set the index of B to 42 on A, and under 1·2 on C read 7·77 on D.

Answer: 7·77.

Example—$\sqrt[2]{5·2 \times 3·6}$.

Set the index of B to 5·2 on A, move the cursor to 3·6 on B and read 4·33 on D.

Answer: 4·33.

Cubes and Cube Roots.

As was stated earlier the K scale is composed of 3 scales, each similar to the D scale, placed end to end. Therefore if the cursor is placed over any number on the D scale, it will cut the K scale at the number whose log is 3 times the log of that number. That is to say, at the cube of the number.

For example—Set the cursor to 3 on D and read 27 on K.

$$3^3 = 27$$

Set the cursor to 6 on D and read 216 on K.

$$6^3 = 216$$

Similarly, to find the cube root of a number, set the cursor to the number on K and read the cube root on D.

Example—Set the cursor to 64 on K and read 4 on D.

$$\sqrt[3]{64} = 4$$

To find the position of the decimal, or characteristic, of any cube, multiply the characteristic by 3. If the cube lies on the left-hand scale of K this is the characteristic of the cube. If it lies on the middle scale of K add one to this, and if on the right-hand scale add two, to obtain the characteristic.

Example—2^3.

Set the cursor to 2 on D, and read 8 on K.

Characteristic of 2 is 0.

$0 \times 3 = 0$. Since the answer is on the left-hand scale of K this is the characteristic.

$$2^3 = 8$$

Example—30^3.

Set the cursor to 3 on D and read 27 on K (middle scale).

Characteristic is then $(1 \times 3) + 1 = 4$.

$$30^3 = 27000$$

Example—$\cdot 08^3$.

Set the cursor to 8 on D and read 512 on K (right-hand scale).

Characteristic is $(-2 \times 3) + 2 = -4$.

$$\cdot 08^3 = \cdot 000512$$

C

Cube Roots.

If the characteristic is positive, divide it by 3, and the result, ignoring any remainder, is the characteristic of the cube root. If the remainder was zero, set on the left-hand scale of K, if remainder was one, on the middle scale of K, and if two on the right-hand scale of K.

For example—$\sqrt[3]{1330}$.

Characteristic is $3 \div 3 = 1$, remainder zero.

Set the cursor to 133 on K, left-hand scale, and read 11·0 on D.

$$\sqrt[3]{1330} = 11$$
$$\sqrt[3]{\overline{1}33}$$

Characteristic is $2 \div 3 = 0$, remainder 2.

Set the cursor to 133 on K, right-hand scale, and read 5·1 on D.

$$\sqrt[3]{133} = 5 \cdot 1$$

If the characteristic is negative, increase it to a multiple of 3 and divide by 3, the result is the characteristic of the cube root. If the characteristic was already a multiple of 3, set on the left-hand scale of K, if it had to be increased by 1, on the middle scale of K, and if by 2 on the right-hand scale of K.

For example—$\sqrt[3]{0 \cdot 125}$.

Characteristic $= -1$, increase to $\dfrac{-3}{3} = -1$.

The original characteristic was increased by 2. Set the cursor to 125 on the right-hand scale of K and read 5 on D.

$$\sqrt[3]{0 \cdot 125} = 0 \cdot 5$$

Example—$\sqrt[3]{\cdot 0034}$.

Characteristic $= -2$. $\therefore \dfrac{-2-1}{3} = -1$.

Increase -1.

Set the cursor to 34 on the middle scale of K and read 324 on D.

$$\sqrt[3]{\cdot0034} = \cdot324$$

Logarithms.

The characteristic is of course found in the normal way by inspection.

To find the Mantissa.

Set the cursor to the number on D and read the log on the L scale.

Example—To find the log of 30.

Characteristic of 30 is 1.

Set the cursor to 3 on D and read ·477 on L.

$$\text{Log}_{10}30 = 1\cdot477$$

To find the Antilog.

Example—$\text{Log}_{10}x = 3\cdot301$.

Characteristic is 3, and mantissa is ·301.

Set the cursor to ·301 on L and read 2 on D.

$$x = 2000$$

Quadratic Equations.

These can be solved simply and rapidly by means of the slide rule.

Reduce the equation to the form:

$$x^2+ax+b = 0.$$

Set the index of C to b on D, move the cursor till it cuts the Cl and D scales at numbers of which the sum or difference is equal to a.

The sum if $+b$ and difference if $-b$.

These two numbers are the roots of the equation.

For example—To solve $x^2+5x+6 = 0$.

Set the index of C to 6 on D. Move the cursor till it cuts 2 on C1 and 3 on D. $(2+3 = 5)$.

$\therefore x^2+5x+6 = (x+2)(x+3) = 0$.

$$x = -2 \text{ or } -3$$

To solve $x^2-7x-11 = 0$.

Set the index of C to 11 on D. Move the cursor slowly and find $8\cdot322$ on C1 and $1\cdot322$ on D $(8\cdot322-1\cdot322 = 7)$.

$\therefore x^2-7x-11 = (x-8\cdot322)(x+1\cdot322) = 0$.

$$x = +8\cdot322 \text{ or } -1\cdot322$$

CHAPTER III

PROPORTIONS AND PERCENTAGES

Any simple proportion problem can be worked quickly and easily on the slide rule, using either A and B scales or the C and D scales with CF and DF.

The A and B scales are sometimes handier, as all settings and readings are made on the same scales, but C and D scales give a better accuracy.

The ordinary problem is often written thus:

M : N :: X : Y or more simply:

$$\frac{M}{N} = \frac{X}{Y}$$

On the slide rule, if M on C is set to N on D, then at X on C (or CF) read Y on D (or DF).

Example—A vessel steams at 17 knots. To find the distance travelled in 25 minutes and the time taken to travel 23 miles:

17 knots = 17 miles in 60 minutes.

$$\frac{17}{60} = \frac{Distance}{Time}$$

Set 60 on C to 17 on D. Then over 25 on CF read 7·08 miles on DF, and over 23 miles on D read 81·2 minutes on C.

Distance 7·08 miles.

Time taken 81·2 minutes.

Example—A vessel covers 12·6 miles in 41 minutes. To find her speed and the distance covered in 71 minutes, also the time required to cover 9 miles.

Set 41 minutes on C to 12·6 miles on D. Then under
60 minutes on C read 18·4 miles on D. Under 71 minutes
on C read 21·8 miles on D. Under 9 miles on DF read
29·3 minutes on CF.

> Speed 18·4 knots.
> Covers 21·8 miles in 71 minutes.
> Covers 9 miles in 29·3 minutes.

Example—In 17 hours a vessel covers 210 miles and
burns 33 tons of fuel. To find:

(*a*) The daily consumption.
(*b*) Time taken to burn 89 tons of fuel.
(*c*) The fuel required for 670 miles.
(*d*) The distance covered on 490 tons of fuel.
(*e*) Vessel's speed.
(*f*) The day's run.

(*a*) and (*b*). Time *v*. Fuel.

Set 17 hours on C to 33 tons on D. Under 24 hours on
C read 46·5 on D. Over 89 tons on D read 45·8 hours
on C.

> Daily consumption 46·5 tons.
> Burns 89 tons in 45·8 hours.

(*c*) and (*d*). Fuel *v*. Distance.

Set 33 tons on C to 210 miles on D. Under 490 tons on
C read 3120 miles on D. Under 670 on DF read 105·2
tons on CF.

> Require 105·2 tons for 670 miles.
> Covers 3120 miles on 490 tons.

(*e*) and (*f*). Time *v*. Distance.

Set 17 hours on C to 210 miles on D. Under 1 hour on
C read 12·33 knots on D. Under 24 hours on C read
296 miles on D.

> Speed 12·33 knots.
> Day's Run 296 miles.

Inverse Proportion.

The simplest method of working these is to use the C1 and D scales on the reverse of the rule. One or two examples will best show how to use them.

Example—It takes 4 men 24 days to complete a certain job. How long would it take 7 men? And how many men would be required to complete it in 16 days?

Set 4 (men) on C1, over 24 (days) on D.

To do this set the cursor to 24 on D and then set 4 on C1 to the cursor. This gives men on C1 and days on D. Move the cursor to 7 (men) on C1 and read 13·7 (days) on D. Now move the cursor to 16 (days) on D and read 6 (men) on C1.

7 men take 13·7 days.

To complete in 16 days, takes 6 men.

Example—A ship steaming at 14 knots can reach her destination in $6\frac{1}{2}$ hours. At what speed must she steam to arrive in $4\frac{3}{4}$ hours?

Set 6·5 (hours) on C1, over 14 (knots) on D. Then under 4·75 (hours) on C1 read 19·15 (knots) on D.

Speed 19·15 knots.

Example—A vessel wishes to load 115 tons of cargo 82 feet forward of the Tipping Centre. At what distance aft of the Tipping Centre must a consignment of 152 tons be loaded, in order to maintain her present Trim?

Set 82 (feet) on C1, over 115 (tons) on D. Move the cursor to 152 (tons) on D and read 62 (feet) on C1.

62 feet abaft the Tipping Centre.

Percentages.

These are only particular cases of proportion.

Example—A vessel steams 432 miles, while her log shows 448 miles. Find the percentage error of the log.

$$448 - 432 = 16.$$

The problem then is: If the error is 16 on 448, what is it on 100?

Set 16 on B to 448 on A and under the index of A (100) read 3·57 on B.

Error 3·57%

Example—A ship's log reads 3·4 per cent fast. What is the distance run when it reads 364?

That is to say on 100 it is 3·4 fast. What will be the error on 364?

Set 100 (index) on B to 3·4 on A. Then over 364 on B read 12·4 on A.

Error 12·4 miles.

∴ True distance = 364 − 12·4 = 351·6 miles.

Alternatively—3·4 per cent fast means that when the log shows 100 the true distance is 100 − 3·4 or 96·6 miles.

Set 100 (log distance) on B to 96·6 (true distance) on A, then over 364 (log) on B, read 352 on A.

True distance 352 miles.

The second method does not give quite the same accuracy as the other, but is normally sufficiently accurate for all practical purposes.

CHAPTER IV

USING THE TRIGONOMETRICAL SCALES

ANY problems involving Trig. Ratios, i.e. Sines, Cosines and Tangents, can be worked on the slide rule, just as simply and in exactly the same way, as ordinary numerical calculations.

As has already been shown, the trig. scales are logarithmic scales, similar to the C and D scales and constructed to the same scale.

It would be possible to convert any trig. ratio to its numerical value and use this number on the C and D scales.

For example—To multiply, say, $4 \times \sin 30$. Sin $30 = 0.5$.

Set the index of C to 4 on D, move the cursor to .5 on C and read 2 on D.

Using the S scale. The sines are marked in plain figures and cosines are in brackets.

Set the index of C to 4 on D, move the cursor to sin $30°$ on S and it cuts the D scale at 2.

It will be seen therefore that any problems involving these ratios can be worked without having to find the numerical value of the ratio. This saves endless time and many possible errors.

Since there are no trig. scales on the rule itself, but only on the slide, the device of centering the slide is resorted to. This means setting the index of the slide coincident with the index of the rule. By this means, when the cursor is moved to any ratio on the trig. scales, it is set to that ratio on the rule, or when the cursor is set to any number on the rule, by centering the slide, it will cut the trig. scale at the equivalent angle.

Centre the slide and set the cursor to sin 20°, that is to say, set the cursor to the 20 on the S scale, and it will cut the D scale at 342.

Sin 20 = 0·342.

Therefore, if it is required to multiply sin 20 by say 2, it is possible to centre the slide, set the cursor to sin 20, set the index of C to the cursor, and under 2 on C read $2 \times$ sin 20 or ·685 on D.

In practice, in this case it is simpler to set the index of C to 2 on D, move the cursor to sin 20 on S and read ·685 on D.

On the slide are found the TA and TB scales, scales of Tangents, the ST scale, a scale of sines and tangents of small angles, and the S scale, a scale of sines and cosines. The sine scale reading from left to right, and cosine scale from right to left, the figures being shewn in brackets. These two scales will be referred to as the sine scale of S and cosine scale of S respectively. When it is required to use these scales, sin θ on S, means use the sine scale, and cos θ on S means use the cosine scale.

It will have been noticed that only sines, cosines and tangents are marked on the slide rule. These are all that are required since

$$\text{Cosec } \theta = \frac{1}{\sin \theta} \quad \sec \theta = \frac{1}{\cos \theta} \quad \text{and cot } \theta = \frac{1}{\tan \theta}$$

That is to say that to multiply by cosec θ one can divide by sin θ, and to divide by cosec θ, multiply by sin θ, etc.

Characteristics of the Ratios.

Sines and cosines on the S Scale – – –1 or $\bar{1}$
Tangents on the TA Scale – – – –1 or $\bar{1}$
Tangents on the TB Scale – – – 0
Sines, cosines and tangents on the ST Scale –2 or $\bar{2}$
Secants and cosecants on the S scale – 0
Cotangents on the TA scale – – 0
Cotangents on the TB scale – – –1 or $\bar{1}$
Secants, cosecants and cotangents on the
ST Scale – – – – – 1

To find the Ratios of Angles.

Centre the slide and set the cursor to the required angle on the appropriate scale, then under the cursor read the ratio on D or the log ratio on L.

To find sin 25°—Centre the slide and set the cursor to sin 25 on S. Under the cursor read ·422 on D and ·626 on L.

Sin 25° = 0·422.

Log sin 25° = $\bar{1}$·626.

To find tan 30°.

Centre the slide and move the cursor to 30 on TA, then under the cursor read ·578 on D and ·762 on L.

Tan 30° = 0·578.

Log tan 30 = $\bar{1}$·762.

To find tan 54°.

Centre the slide and move the cursor to 54 on TB and under the cursor read 1·376 on D and ·139 on L.

Tan 54° = 1·376.

Log tan 54 = 0·139.

To find cos 57°.

Centre the slide, move the cursor to 57° on the cosine scale of S, and read ·545 on D and ·736 on L.

$$\text{Cos } 57° \quad = 0·545.$$
$$\text{Log cos } 57 \quad = \bar{1}·736$$

To find sin 2° 37′.

Centre the slide, move the cursor to 2° 37′ on ST and read ·0457 on D and ·660 on L.

$$\text{Sin } 2° \ 37′ \quad = 0·0457.$$
$$\text{Log sin } 2° \ 37′ \quad = \bar{2}·66.$$

To find tan 1° 42′.

Centre the slide, move the cursor to 1° 42′ on ST and read ·0297 on D and ·473 on L.

$$\text{Tan } 1° \ 42′ \quad = 0·0297.$$
$$\text{Log tan } 1° \ 42′ \quad = \bar{2}·473.$$

Note that here the same scale has been used for both sines and tangents. For angles on less than 6° the difference between the sine and tangent is so small that, for practical purposes, they may be assumed to be the same.

To find the cosecant of 30°.

$$\text{Cosec } 30 = \frac{1}{\sin 30}$$

Set the cursor to 1 (the index) on D, then set 30 on the sine scale of S to the cursor, move the cursor to the index of C and read 2 on D and ·301 on L.

$$\text{Cosec } 30° \quad = 2·0.$$
$$\text{Log cosec } 30° \quad = 0·301.$$

Here we have divided 1 by sin 30.

Similarly with the other ratios.

To find cot 40°.

Move the cursor to the index of D and set 40° on TA to the cursor, then under the index of C read 1·19 on D and ·076 on L.

Cot 40° = 1·19.
Log cot 40° = 0·076.

In practice, as has been previously explained, one seldom needs to read the ratio when using the slide rule. A few examples should make this clear.

Solve 7 . sin 47—Set the index of C to 7 on D, move the cursor to sin 47 on S and read 5·12 on D.

7 . sin 47 = 5·12.

Notice here that 7 has been multiplied by sin 47 without reading the value of sin 47.

Solve 42 . tan 61° 40'—Set the index of C to 42 on D, move the cursor to 61° 40' on TB and read 78 on D.

42 . tan 61° 40' = 78.

Solve 21 . cos 50° 30'—Set the index of C to 21 on D, move the cursor to cos 50° 30' (figures in brackets) on S, and read 13·37 on D.

21 . cos 50° 30' = 13·37.

Solve 18 . cosec 26° 40'—Set the cursor to 18 on D and set sin 26° 40' on S to the cursor, then under the index of C read 40·1 on D.

18 . cosec 26° 40' = 40·1.

As can be seen the method used here has been to divide 18 by sin 26° 40'.

Solve 43·2 . sec 48° 20'—Set the cursor to 43·2 on D and set cos 48° 20' (figures in brackets) on S to the cursor, then under the index of C read 65 on D.

43·2 . sec 48° 20' = 65.

Here again the method is to divide 43·2 by cos 48° 20′.

Solve 37.cot 28° 10′—Set the cursor to 37 on D, and set 28° 10′ on TA to the cursor, then, under the index of C read 69·1 on D.

37.cot 28° 10′ = 69·1.

Solve 24·4.cot 59°—Set the cursor to 24·4 on D and set 59° on TB to the cursor, then under the index of C read 14·66 on D.

24·4.cot 59° = 14·66.

Solve 3·8.sin 3° 21′—Set the index of C to 3·8 on D, move the cursor to 3° 21′ on ST and read 0·222 on D.

3·8.sin 3° 21′ = 0·222.

Solve 41.cot 2° 43′—Set the cursor to 41 on D and set 2° 43′ on ST to the cursor, then under the index of C read 865 on D.

41.cot 2° 43′ = 865.

Solve $\tan \theta = \dfrac{45}{67}$ —Set the index of C to 67 on D, move the cursor to 45 on D and under the cursor read 33° 52′ on TA.

$\theta = 33° 52′$.

If the characteristic is −1 read on TA, 0 on TB or −2 on ST.

Alternative Setting.

Set 67 on C over 45 on D, move the cursor to the index of C. Centre the slide and under the cursor read 33° 52′ on TA.

The first method is simpler, as it saves having to centre the slide.

Solve $\tan \theta = \dfrac{67}{45}$ —Set the index of C to 45 on D, move the cursor to 67 on D and read 56° 08′ on TB.

$\theta = 56° 08′$.

Since the characteristic is 0, scale TB is used.

Solve $\sin \theta = \dfrac{17}{47}$ —Set the index of C to 47 on D, move the cursor to 17 on D and read 21° 07′ on the sine scale of S.

$\theta = 21° 16′$.

Solve $\sin \theta = \dfrac{2}{85}$ —Characteristic −2. Use ST scale.

Set the index of C to 85 on D, move the cursor to 2 on D and read 1° 21′ on ST.

$\theta = 1° 21′$.

Solve $\sin \theta = \sin 24° 20′ \times \sec 51° 40′$.

This could be written: $\sin \theta = \dfrac{\sin 24° 20′}{\cos 51° 40′}$

Centre the slide. Move the cursor to $\sin 24° 20′$ on S, set $\cos 51° 40′$ to the cursor, move the cursor to the index of C. Centre the slide, and read 41° 35′ on the sine scale of S.

$\theta = 41° 35′$.

Alternative Setting.

Set $\cos 51° 40′$ on S over the index of D, move the cursor to $\sin 24° 20′$ on S. Centre the slide, and read 41° 35′ on the sine scale of S.

$\theta = 41° 35′$.

Solve $\tan \theta = \tan 40° 15′$. Cos 37° 20′—Centre the slide. Move the cursor to 40° 15′ on TA, set the index of C to the cursor, move the cursor to cos 37° 20′ on S. Centre the slide and read 33° 57′ on TA.

$\theta = 33° 57′.$

Solve cos θ = sin 27° 20′. Tan 56° 30′.

Centre the slide. Move the cursor to sin 27° 20′ on S, set the index of C to the cursor, move the cursor to 56° 30′ on TB. Centre the slide and read 46° 05′ on the cos scale of S.

$\theta = 46° 05′.$

Solve cosec θ = tan 61° 40′. Cos 15° 30′.

Centre the slide. Move the cursor to 61° 40′ on TB, set the index of C to the cursor, move the cursor to cos 15° 30′ on S. Set the index of C to the cursor, move the cursor to the index of D, and read 34° 00′ on the sine scale of S.

$\theta = 34° 00′.$

Solve cot θ = sin 30° 40′. Cot 65° 20′.

Set 65° 20′ on TB over the index of D, move the cursor to sin 30° 40′ on S. Set the index of C to the cursor and over the index of D read 23° 08′ on TA.

$\theta = 23° 08′.$

If the characteristic is 0 read on TB, if −1 (1) on TA.

For the beginner it is often helpful to rewrite any problem using only sin, cos and tan.

Thus, it is required to solve:

$x = $ sin 22° 40′, sec 41° 30′, cot 62° 20′, cos 57° 00′.

Rewrite as:

$$x = \frac{\text{Sin } 22° \ 40' \times \cos 75° \ 00'}{\cos 41° \ 30' \times \tan 62° \ 20'}$$

Set cos 41° 30′ on S to the index of D, move the cursor to sin 22° 40′ on S, set 62° 40′ on TB to the cursor and move the cursor to cos 75 on S then under the cursor read ·0698 on D.

$$x = ·0698.$$

D

CHAPTER V

CARGO WORK, STABILITY AND TRIM

WHEN the ship is in port a slide rule is more than a useful time-saver, it is practically indispensable. There are an infinite number of calculations, such as space required to stow a consignment of any cargo, capacity of holds and tanks, space remaining in a compartment, trim and stability calculations, safe working loads and many others, that can all be worked rapidly and very simply on the slide rule.

In this chapter some of the typical problems are explained. Once the user has started handling a slide rule, he will find that a hundred and one calculations are made daily and will use the rule more and more.

The Space Remaining in a Hold or Compartment.

Cargo space is normally taken at 40 cu. ft. per ton.

$$\therefore \text{Space at 40 cu. ft./ton} = \frac{L \times B \times D}{40}$$

Either A and B or C and D scales are used.

Set the index of C to L on D, move the cursor to B on C, set 40 on C to the cursor and under D on C, read the space at 40 cu. ft./ton on D.

Example—Length 18 ft., breadth 9 ft. 6 in., height 5 ft. 3 in.

Set the index of C to 18 on D, move the cursor to 9·5 on C and set 40 on C to the cursor. Then under 5·25 on C read 22·4 on D.

Space = 22·4 tons at 40 cu. ft./ton.

Example—A compartment measures 30 ft. × 24 ft. × 8 ft. 6 in.   How many tons of goods stowing at 53 cu. ft./ton will it take?

Set the index of C to 30 on D, move the cursor to 24 on C, set 53 on C to the cursor and under 8·5 on C read 115 on D.

Space takes 115 tons at 53 cu. ft./ton.

In this case it was necessary to reset the slide to make the final reading.   This could have been avoided by using scales A and B.

Example—A compartment will hold 240 tons of cargo at 40 cu. ft./ton.   How many tons of cargo stowing at 57 cu. ft./ton will it take?

This is inverse proportion.

Use scales C1 and D.

Set the cursor to 40 on D and set 240 on C1 to the cursor.   Move the cursor to 57 on D and read 168·5 on C1.

Takes 168·5 tons at 57 cu. ft./tons.

Or using C and D scales.

$$\text{Tons taken} = \frac{240 \times 04}{57}$$

Set 57 on C over 240 on D and under 40 on C read 168·5 on D.

168·5 tons.

Example—What space at 40 cu. ft./ton is required to stow 1200 tons of soya beans stowing at 55 cu. ft./ton?

Set 55 on C1 over 1200 on D, move the cursor to 40 on C1, and read 1650 on D.

1650 tons space at 40 cu. ft./ton.

Or using C and D scales

$$\text{Space required} = \frac{1200 \times 55}{40}$$

Set 40 on C over 1200 on D, move the cursor to 55 on C and read 1650 on D.

1650 tons.

Similarly, using Specific Gravities.

A tank can hold 550 tons of salt-water at S.G. 1·025. To find the tons of oil at S.G. 0·91.

Set 1·025 on CF to 550 on DF. Over 0·91 on CF read 488 tons on DF.

488 tons of oil.

To find the Weight of a Fir Log at 38 lb./cu. ft.

Length 40 ft., breadth 15 in., depth 18 in.

Weight = $40 \times 1·25 \times 1·5 \times 38$ lb.

Set the index of C to 40 on D, move the cursor to 1·25 on C, set 1·5 on C1 to the cursor and under 38 on C read 2850 lb. on D.

Weight = 2850 lb.

To find the Volume of a Cylinder.

Vol. = $\frac{\pi}{4} D^2 L$. or $\left(\sqrt{\frac{\pi}{4}} D \right)^2 L$.

On the C and D scales will be found a mark 'C' at about 1·13.

This mark is at the reciprocal of $\sqrt{\dfrac{\pi}{4}}$ or $\dfrac{1}{\sqrt{\dfrac{\pi}{4}}}$

Set 'C' on C over the diameter on D and over the length on B read the volume on A.

Example—To find the volume of cylinder, diameter 18 in., length 12 ft.

Set 'C' on C over 1·5 ft. (18 in.) on D and over 12 on B read 21·2 on A.

Volume 21·2 cu. ft.

To find the Weight of an Elm Log (35 lb./cu. ft.).

Length 22 ft., mean diameter 21 in.

21 in. = 1·75 ft.

Set 'C' on C over 1·75 on D, move the cursor to 22 on B, set the index of B to the cursor and over 35 on B read 1845 on A.

Weight 1845 lb.

Safe Working Loads

Manila Rope.

For a single Lift $\text{SWL} = \dfrac{C^2}{7}$

For continuous running $\text{SWL} = \dfrac{C^2}{18}$

Where SWL is in tons, and C the circumference in inches.

For single lift—Set the cursor to C on D and set 7 on B to the cursor. Then over the index of B read the SWL on A.

For continuous running—Set the cursor to C on D and set 18 on B to the cursor, then over the index of B read the SWL on A.

Example—To find the SWL of a 3½-in. fall.

Set the cursor to 3·5 on D, set 18 on B to the cursor, and over the index of B read 0·68 on A.

SWL = 0·68 ton or 13½ cwt.

To find the size of rope for a given lift (single lift).

$C^2 = \text{Lift} \times 7$ or $C = \sqrt{\text{Lift} \times 7}$.

Set the index of B to the lift on A, move the cursor to 7 on B and read the size of rope on D.

Example—What size rope must be used to lift a case weighing $1\frac{1}{2}$ ton?

Set the index of B to 1·5 on A, move the cursor to 7 on B and read 3·25 on D.

$3\frac{1}{4}$-in. rope required.

Example—What size of rope fall must be used when working with a load of 12 cwt?

12 cwt = 0·6 ton.

Set the index of B to 0·6 on A, move the cursor to 18 on B and read 3·28 on D.

Use $3\frac{1}{4}$-in. or $3\frac{1}{2}$-in. rope fall.

To find number of parts of a smaller rope to equal a larger rope.

$$\frac{\text{No. of parts of the smaller}}{\text{No. of parts of the larger}} = \frac{C^2 \text{ of smaller}}{C^2 \text{ of larger}}$$

Set the size of the smaller rope on C over the size of the larger rope on D, then over the index of B read the number of parts on A.

Example—To find the number of parts of $\frac{3}{4}$-in. rope to equal a 2-in. rope, set 0·75 on C over 2 on D and over the index of B read 7·1 on A.

Over 7 parts, so 8 parts are needed.

Wire Ropes.

$$\text{SWL in tons} = \frac{\text{breaking strain}}{6}$$

Breaking strain of wire-rope.
6-strand, 12 wires per strand = $2 C^2$
6-strand, 24 wires per strand = $3 C^2$
6-strand, 37 wires per strand = $3\frac{1}{4} C^2$
Safe working loads.

6-strand, 12 wires per strand = $\dfrac{C^2}{3}$

6-strand, 24 wires per strand = $\dfrac{C^2}{2}$

6-strand, 37 wires per strand = $\dfrac{3 \cdot 25\, C^2}{6}$

To find the SWL of $2\frac{1}{2}$-in. wire (24 wires).

Set the cursor to 2·5 on D and set 2 on B to the cursor.
Then over the index of B read 3·1 on A.

SWL = 3·1 ton.

To find the SWL of $2\frac{1}{4}$-in. wire (37 wires).

Move the cursor to 2·25 on D. Set 6 on B to the cursor
and over 3·25 on B read 2·75 on A.

SWL = 2·75 ton.

To find the size of wire required for a given stress.

6-strand, 12 wires per strand, $C^2 = 3 \times$ stress,
$$C = \sqrt{3 \times \text{stress}}$$

6-strand, 24 wires per strand, $C^2 = 2 \times$ stress,
$$C = \sqrt{2 \times \text{stress}}$$

6-strand, 37 wires per strand, $C^2 = \dfrac{6 \times \text{stress}}{3 \cdot 25}$

$$C = \frac{\sqrt{6 \times \text{stress}}}{3 \cdot 25}$$

To find the size of wire required for a load of $1\frac{1}{2}$ ton, the wire having 24 wires per strand. Set the index of B to 1·5 on A, move the cursor to 2 on B and read 1·73 on D.

$1\frac{3}{4}$-in. wire is required.

To find the size of wire (37-strand) required for a stress of $2\frac{1}{4}$-ton.

Set 3·25 on B to 6 on A, move the cursor to 2·25 on B and read 2·04 on D.

∴ $2\frac{1}{4}$-in. wire required.

SWL of Chains.

SWL = $6d^2$.

Where SWL is in tons, d is the diameter in inches of the metal forming the link.

To find SWL.

Set the index of C to the diameter on D and over 6 on B read the SWL on A.

Example—To find the SWL of a $\frac{3}{4}$-in. chain.

Set the index of C to 0·75 on D and over 6 on B read 3·36 on A.

SWL = 3·36 ton.

To find the size of a chain for a given stress.

$$d^2 = \frac{\text{stress}}{6}, \quad d = \sqrt{\frac{\text{stress}}{6}}$$

Set 6 on B under the stress on A and under the index of C read the size of chain on D.

Example—What size chain is required for a load of 4 tons?

Set 6 on B to 4 on A and under the index of C read ·815 on D.

Nearest size $\frac{7}{8}$ ft. (·875 in.).

A good approximation of the SWL may be found by taking the (diameter in $\frac{1}{8}$-in.)$^2 \div 10$.

Thus in the example above.

To find SWL of a $\frac{3}{4}$-in. chain.

$$\frac{3}{4} = \frac{6}{8}$$

$$\frac{6^2}{10} = 3·6$$

This gives a SWL of 3·6 ton by the approximate formula as against 3·36 ton by the correct formula.

Trim Problems.

Change of trim $= \dfrac{\text{moment to change trim}}{\text{inch-trim moment}}$

Set I.T.M. on C over the moment to change trim on D and under the index of C read the change of trim on D.

Example—Given I.T.M. = 950. To find the change of trim when 400 ton is loaded 114 ft. from the tipping centre.

$$\therefore \text{Change of trim} = \frac{400 \times 114}{950}$$

Set 950 on C over 400 on D, move the cursor to 114 on C and read 48 on D.

Change of Trim = 48 in.

This could have been worked on the A and B scales and thus save resetting the slide.

Set 950 on B under 400 on A and over 114 on B read 48 on A.

Change of trim = 48 in.

When the tipping centre is not at the $\frac{1}{2}$ length of the vessel, the change of draft at each end of the vessel is proportional the distance of the tipping centre from either end.

Example—A vessel 350 ft. in length loads 210 ton, 64 ft. forward of the tipping centre, which is 6 ft. forward of the middle length. I.T.M. 1120, T.P.I. 48.

If the original draft was 20 ft. 6 in. forward, and 21 ft. 9 in. aft, what will be her new draft?

$$\text{Sinkage} = \frac{210}{48} \left(\frac{\text{weight loaded}}{\text{T.P.I.}} \right)$$

Set 48 on C over 210 on D and under the index of C read 4·4 on D.

Sinkage 4·4 in.

Tipping centre lies 181 ft. $\left(\frac{350}{2} + 6 \right)$ from aft and 169 ft. $\left(\frac{350}{2} - 6 \right)$ from forward.

$\therefore$ Change of draft aft $= \dfrac{210 \times 64}{1120} \times \dfrac{181}{350}$

Change of draft forward $= \dfrac{210 \times 64}{1120} \times \dfrac{169}{350}$

To avoid having to reset the slide this may be worked either using A and B scales or C, D and C1.

Using A and B.

Set 1120 on B to 210 on A, move the cursor to 64 on B, and set 350 on B to the cursor, then over 181 on B read 6·2 on A and over 169 on B read 5·8 on A.

Using C, D, CF and DF.

Set 1120 on C to 210 on D, move the cursor to 64 on CF, and set 350 on CF to the cursor. Under 181 on C read 6·2 on D, and under 169 on C read 5·8 on D.

Ch. of dr. aft = 6·2 in.   Ch. of dr. for'd = 5·8 in.
Original draft 20 ft. 6 in.   For'd 21 ft. 9 in. aft.

Sinkage		4·4			4·4
	20	10·4		22	1·4
Trim	+	5·8		−	6·2
Final draft	21	4·2 For'd		21	7·2 aft

To find the Moment to alter trim one inch. (I.T.M.)

$$I.T.M. = \frac{30T^2}{B}$$

Where T is Tons per inch immersion, and
   B is the Moulded Breadth.

Set the cursor to T on D, set Breadth, on B, to the cursor and over 30 on B read the I.T.M. on A.

Example—Required the I.T.M. Given moulded breadth 58 ft. and T.P.I. 49 tons.

Set the cursor to 49 on D and set 58 on B to the cursor, then over 30 on B read 1240 on A.

   I.T.M. = 1240.

Using Longitudinal Metacentre.

$$I.T.M. = \frac{W \times GM_L}{12L}$$

Where GM_L is the Longitudinal Metacentre.

   W is the Displacement.

   L is the Length of the vessel.

Set 12 on C over W on D, move the cursor to GM_L on C and set L on C to the cursor, then under the index of C read the I.T.M. on D.

Example—Required the I.T.M. given displacement 11,700 ton, length 384 ft., GM_L 449 ft.

$$\therefore \text{I.T.M.} = \frac{11,700 \times 449}{12 \times 384}$$

Set 12 on C over 11,700 on D, move the cursor to 449 on C, set 384 on C to the cursor and under the index of C read 1140 on D.

I.T.M. = 1140.

Change of draft due to Heel.

Ch. of dr. $= \frac{1}{2}$ Breadth $\times$ sine angle of heel—rise of floor.

Example—Breadth 48 ft. Heel 4°, rise of floor 9 in.

Set the index of C to 24 on D, move the cursor to 4° on ST and read 1·67 on D, set the index of C to the cursor and under 12 on C read 20 on D.

Ch. of dr. = 20in. (or 1·67ft.)—9in. = 11in.
Ch. of draft = 11 in.

To find the Fresh-water Allowance.

$$\text{F.W.A.} = \frac{W}{40 \times \text{T.P.I.}}$$

Set 40 on C to the index of D, move the cursor to W on C, set T.P.I. on C to the cursor and under the index of C read the F.W.A. on D.

Example—Displacement 12,200 tons. T.P.I. 49·5 tons.

Set 40 on C to the index of D, move the cursor to 12,200 on C, set 49·5 on C to the cursor and under the index of C read 6·16 on D.

F.W.A. = 6·16 in.

To find the change of draft going from water of one density to water of another density.

Ch. of dr. $= \dfrac{W \times \text{change of S.G.}}{\text{T.P.I.}}$

Set T.P.I. on C over W on D, move the cursor to the change of S.G. on C and read the ch. of dr. on D.

Example—Find change of draft proceeding from sea-water (S.G. 1·025) to river-water (S.G. 1·007). Displacement 8750 tons, T.P.I. 47.

Set 47 on C over 8750 on D, and under ·018 (1·025—1·007) on C read 3·35 on D.

Ch. of draft = 3·35 in.

Given F.W.A. to find the change of draft.

Ch. of dr. $= \dfrac{\text{F.W.A.} \times \text{change of S.G.}}{·025}$

Example—F.W.A. 6·5 in. S.G. of river-water 1·010.

Set ·025 on C over 6·5 on D and under 0·015 (1·025—1·010) on C read 3·9 on D.

Ch. of draft = 3·9 in.

Given F.W.A., draft and maximum draft.

To find the change of draft going from salt-water to fresh-water.

Ch. of dr. $= \dfrac{\text{F.W.A.} \times \text{draft}}{\text{max. draft}}$

This is an approximate formula, but quite accurate enough for practical purposes.

Example—F.W.A. 9 in., draft 22 ft. 6 in., max. draft 29 ft. 3 in.

Set 29·25 on C over 9 on D and under 22·5 on C read 6·9 on D.

Ch. of draft = 6·9 in.

To find the change of draft going from salt-water to river-water.

$$\text{Ch. of dr.} = \frac{\text{F.W.A.} \times \text{draft}}{\text{max. draft}} \times \frac{\text{Change of S.G.}}{\cdot 025}$$

Example—F.W.A. 8 in., draft 20 ft. 6 in., max. draft 30 ft. 6 in. S.G. of river-water 1·007.

Set 30·5 on C over 8 on D, move the cursor to 20·5 on C, set ·025 on C to the cursor, and under ·018 (1·025 —1·007) on C read 3·87 on D.

Ch. of draft = 3·87 in.

Stability Calculations.

$$GG_1 = \frac{w \times d}{W}$$

Example—Vessel of displacement 8550 tons, a weight of 70 tons was moved transversely, through 22 ft. Find the shift of G.

$$\therefore GG_1 = \frac{70 \times 22}{8550}$$

Set 8550 on C over 70 on D and under 22 on C read ·180 on D.

$GG_1 = \cdot 180$ ft.

$GM = GG_1 \cot \theta$

Example—Given GG_1 as ·08. Heel = 4°.

Set 4° on S T over ·08 on D, then under the index of C read 1·145 on D.

$GM = 1·145$ ft.

$$GM = \frac{w \times d}{W. \tan \theta}$$

Example—Displacement 11,000 tons. A weight of 20 tons moved 36 ft. athwartships, heeled the vessel through 5°. Find the GM.

Set 11,000 on C over 20 on D, move the cursor to 36 on C and set 5° on S T to the cursor, then under the index of C read ·75 on D.

GM = 0·75 ft.

GZ = GM sin θ.

Example—Given GM 2·3 ft., find the GZ at $3°\frac{1}{2}$ heel.

Set the index of C to 2·3 on D, move the cursor to 3° 30′ on S T and read ·14 on D.

GZ = 0·14 ft.

$$\text{Tan } θ = \frac{GG_1}{GM}$$

Example—GG_1 0·15 ft.   GM 2·2 ft.

Set the index of C to 2·2 on D, move the cursor to ·15 on D and read 3° 54′ on S T.

Heel = 3° 54′.

$$\text{Tan } θ = \frac{W \times GM}{w \times d}$$

Example—Displacement 9500 tons. A weight of 75 tons moved athwartships through 37 ft. If the GM was 2·4 ft., find the angle of heel.

$$\text{Tan } θ = \frac{75 \times 37}{9500 \times 2·4}$$

Set 9500 on C over 75 on D, move the cursor to 37 on C, set 2·4 on C to the cursor. Move the cursor to the index of C. Centre the slide and read 6° 59′ on T.A.

Angle of heel 6° 59′.

Inclining experiment to find GM.

$$GM = \frac{w \times d}{W} \times \frac{\text{Deflection of plumb-bob}}{\text{Length of plumb-line}}$$

Example—Displacement 12,000 tons, length of plumb-line 22 ft. A weight of 25 tons moved 42 ft. athwartships caused a deflection of 9 inches.

22 ft. = 264 in.

$$GM = \frac{25 \times 42}{12,000} \times \frac{264}{9}$$

Set 12,000 on C over 25 on D, move the cursor to 42 on C, set 9 on C to the cursor and under 264 on C read 2·57 on D.

GM = 2·57 ft.

Virtual rise of G due to free surface.

$$GG^1 = \frac{1}{V} \times \frac{dr}{ds} \times \frac{1}{n^2}$$

This is the exact formula but for practical purposes the following may be used.

$$GG^1 = \frac{lb^3}{420W} \times \frac{1}{n^2}$$

Where l is length of tank

b is breadth of tank

W is displacement of vessel

n is number of longitudinal divisions

Example—To find the virtual rise of G when a tank, 35 ft. in length and 52 ft. breadth, with a centre line bulkhead is slack. Displacement 12,400 ton.

Set 2 (n = 2) on C to 52 (b) on D, move the cursor to 52 on B, set 420 on B to the cursor, move the cursor to 35 (l) on B, set 12,400 on B to the cursor, and over the index of B read 0·237 on A.

Virtual rise of G = 0·237 ft.

CHAPTER VI

NAVIGATION CALCULATIONS

Dead Reckoning and Astronomical

Use as a Traverse Table.

To find D. Lat and Dep.

D. Lat = Distance . cos co.

Dep = Distance . sin co.

Set the index of C to the distance on D, move the cursor to cos co. on S and read the D. Lat on D. Move the cursor to sin co on S and read Dep on D.

Example—Course ·056° T. Distance 81 nm.

Set the index of C to 81 on D, move the cursor to cos 56° on S and read 45·4 on D, move the cursor to sin 56° on S and read 67·2 on D.

D. Lat = 45·4 nm. N.

Dep = 67·2 nm. E.

Example—Course 242° T. Distance 445'.

Set the index of C to 445 on D, move the cursor to cos 62° on S and read 209' on D, move the cursor to sin 62° on S and read 393' on D.

D. Lat = 209' S.

Dep = 393' W.

To convert D. Long to Dep.

Dep = D. Long . cos Lat.

Set the index of C to the D. Long on D, move the cursor to cos Lat on S and read the Dep on D.

Example—Lat 31° 30'.   D. Long 50'.

Set the index of C to 50 on D, move the cursor to cos 31° 30' on S and read 42·6 on D.

Dep = 42·6 nm.

To convert Dep to D. Long.

D. Long = Dep . sec Lat.

Set the cursor to the Dep on D, set cos Lat on S to the cursor and under the index of C read the D. Long on D.

Example—Lat 47° 15'.   Dep 171 nm.

Set the cursor to 171 on D, set cos 47° 15' on S to the cursor and under the index of C read 252 on D.

D. Long = 252' = 4° 12'.

Example—Vessel in Lat 48° 30' N., Long 20° 15' W. Steered 034° T. for 212 nm.   Required the D.R. position.

Set the index of C to 212 on D, move the cursor to cos 034 on S and read 176 on D, move the cursor to sin 034 on S and read 118·5 on D.

Lat Dep	48° 30' N.
D. Lat	2° 56' N. (176')
Lat Arr	51° 26' N.
Mean Lat	49° 58' N.

With the cursor still set to 118·5 (Dep) on D, set cos 49° 58' on S to the cursor and under the index of C read 184·5 on D.

Long Dep   20° 15′ W.
D. Long   3°   4·5′ E. (184·5′)
─────────────────────
Long Arr   17° 10·5′ W.

D.R. Position Lat   51° 26′ N.
            Long   17° 10·5′ W.

To find the Course.

$$\text{Tan co} = \frac{\text{Dep}}{\text{D. Lat}}$$

Set the index of C to the D. Lat on D, move the cursor to the Dep on D and under the cursor read the course on TA or TB.

D. Lat greater than Dep on TA.
Dep greater than D. Lat on TB.

Example—D. Lat 40′ N. Dep 26′ E.

Set the index of C to 40 on D, move the cursor to 26 on D and read 33° on TA

Course N. 33° E. = 033° T.

Example—D. Lat 208′ S. Dep 312′ E.

Set the index of C to 208 on D, move the cursor to 312 on D and read 56° 18′ on TB.

Course S 56° 18′ E. = 123° 42′ T.

To find the Distance.

Distance = D. Lat . sec co.

Set the cursor to the D. Lat on D, set cos co on S to the cursor and under the index of C read the distance on D.

Example—D. Lat 45·4.   Course 056° T.

Set the cursor to 45·4 on D, and set cos 56° on S to the cursor, and under the index of C read 81 on D.

Distance = 81 nm.

Example—To find the course and distance from Lat 48° 20′ N., Long 33° 42′ W. to Lat 46° 15′ N., Long 36° 22′ W.

Lat Dep	48° 20′ N.	Long Dep	33° 42′ W.
Lat Arr	46° 15′ N.	Long Arr	36° 22′ W.
D. Lat	2° 5′ S.	D. Long	2° 40′ W.
=	125′	=	160′

To convert D. Long to Dep.

Set the index of C to 160 on D, move the cursor to cos 47° 17½′ (M. Lat) on S and read 108·5 on D.

∴ Dep = 108·5.

To find the Course.

Set the index of C to 125 on D, move the cursor to 108·5 on D and read 41° on TA.

Course = S. 41° W.

To find the Distance.

Set the cursor to 125′ (D. Lat) on D, set cos 41° (course) on S to the cursor, and under the index of C read 165·5 on D.

Distance = 165·5.

Course   = S 41° W. = 221° T.
Distance = 165·5 nm.

To find the True Middle Latitude.

$$\text{Sec Mid Lat} = \frac{\text{DMP}}{\text{D. Lat}}$$

Example—To find the True Mid Lat between 'A' Lat 52° 40′ N and 'B' Lat 46° 35′ N.

From the Table of Mer Parts (Spheroid)

Lat	52° 40′	Mer Parts	3712·03
Lat	46° 35′	Mer Parts	3149·19
D. Lat	6° 05′	DMP	562·84
	= 365′		

Set 365 on C over 562·84 on D. Move the cursor to the index of D and read 49° 30′ on the cos scale of S.

Mid Lat = 49° 30′ N.

Mercator sailing problems may be worked in exactly the same manner, substituting Diff of Mer Parts for D. Lat and D. Long for Dep when finding the course.

$$\text{I.e. } \tan \text{co} = \frac{\text{D. Long}}{\text{DMP}}$$

and Dist = D. Lat . sec co.

It should be borne in mind by the airman that where 'Course' is referred to in these problems, the airman would use the word 'Track'.

Settings for Astronomical Navigation.

To find the Bearing Amplitude.

Sin Amp = Sin Dec . sec Lat.

Set cos Lat on S to the index of D, move the cursor to sin Dec on S, centre the slide, and under the cursor read the amp on the sin scale of S.

Example—Lat 40°, Dec 20°.

Set cos 40° on S to the index of D, move the cursor to sin 20 on S, centre the slide, and under the cursor read 26° 32′ on the sin scale of S.

Bearing amp = 26° 32′.

To find the Time Amplitude.

Sin (Time) Amp = Tan Lat . tan Dec.

Centre the slide, move the cursor to the Lat on TA or TB, set the index of C to the cursor, move the cursor to the Dec on TA or TB, centre the slide and read the Amp on the sin scale of S, at the cursor.

Example—Lat 51° 20′, Dec 14° 30′.

Centre the slide, move the cursor to 51° 20′ on TB, set the index of C to the cursor, move the cursor to 14° 30′ on TA. Centre the slide, and read 18° 50′ on the sin scale of S.

Time Amp = 18° 50′ = 1 hr. 15 min. 20 sec.

To find the Azimuth.

$$\text{Sin Az.} = \frac{\sin \text{HA} \times \cos \text{Dec}}{\cos \text{Alt}}$$

Centre the slide, move the cursor to sin HA on S, set cos Alt on S to the cursor, move the cursor to cos Dec on S. Centre the slide, and under the cursor read the Azimuth on the sin scale of S.

Example—Hour angle 43°, Dec 15°, Altitude 34° 30′.

Centre the slide, move the cursor to sin 43 on S, set cos 34° 30′ on S to the cursor, move the cursor to cos 15° on S, centre the slide and at the cursor read sin 53 on S.

Azimuth 53°.

Alternatively—

Using cosec Az $= \dfrac{\cos \text{Alt}}{\sin \text{HA} \times \cos \text{Dec}}$

Set sin HA on S to the index of D, move the cursor to cos Alt on S, set cos Dec on S to the cursor. Set the cursor to the index of D and read sin Az on S.

In the above example.

Set sin 43 on S to the index of D, move the cursor to cos 34° 30′ on S, set cos 15 to the cursor and over the index of D read sin 53 on S.

Azimuth 53°.

To find the Altitude to set on a Sextant to pick up a Star.

Sec Alt = sin Az . cosec HA . sec Dec.

or $\dfrac{1}{\cos \text{Alt}} = \dfrac{\sin \text{Az}}{\sin \text{HA} \cos \text{Dec}}$

Set sin HA on S over the index of D, move the cursor to sin Azimuth on S, set cos Dec on S to the cursor then over the index of D read the altitude on the cos scale of S.

Example—Hour angle 61° 30′, Azimuth 85°, Declination 21°.

Set sin 61° 30′ on S to the index of D, move the cursor to sin 75° on S, set cos 21° on S to the cursor, and over the index of D read cos 31° 50′ on S.

Altitude 31° 50′.

To find the Altitude of a Body on the Prime Vertical.

Cosec Alt = sin Lat cosec Dec

$$or \quad \frac{1}{\sin Alt} = \frac{\sin Lat}{\sin Dec}$$

Set sin Dec on S to the index of D, move the cursor to sin Lat on S, set the index of C to the cursor and over the index of D read sin Altitude on S.

Example—Lat 52° N., Dec 18 N.

Set sin 18 on S over the index of D, move the cursor to sin 52 on S, set the index of C to the cursor and over the index of D read sin 23° 03′ on S.

Altitude 23° 03′.

To find the Hour Angle of a Body on the Prime Vertical.

Sec HA = tan Lat cot Dec

$$or \quad \frac{1}{\cos HA} = \frac{\tan Lat}{\tan Dec}$$

Set the Dec on TA or TB to the index of D, move the cursor to the Lat on TA or TB, set the index of C to the cursor and over the index of D read cos HA on S.

Example—Lat 48°, Dec 16°.

Set 16° on TA over the index of D, move the cursor to 48° on TB, set the index of C to the cursor and over the index of D read cos 75 on S.

HA = 75° = 5 hrs.

To find the Change of Altitude per Minute of Time.

Change of Alt = 15′ . sin Az cos Lat per minute of time.

Set the index of C to 15 on D, move the cursor to
sin Az on S, set the index of C to the cursor and move
the cursor to cos Lat on S.   Read the change of altitude
on D.

Example—Lat 55°, Azimuth 62°.

Set the index of C to 15 on D, move the cursor to
sin 62 on S, set the index of C to the cursor, move the
cursor to cos 55 on S, and read 7·6 on D.

Change of altitude = 7·6′ per minute.

To find the Error in Longitude due to an Error of 1′ of Latitude.

Error = cot Az sec Lat.

Set cos Lat on S over the index of D, move the cursor
to the index of C and set the Azimuth on TA or TB to the
cursor, and under the index of C read the error on D.

Example—Lat 37° 30′, Azimuth 70°.

Set cos 37° 30′ over the index of D, move the cursor
to the index of C and set 70° on TB to the cursor.   Then
under the index of C read ·46 on D.

Error = 0·46′.

To find the Error in Latitude due to an Error of 1′ Longitude.

Error = tan Az cos Lat.

Centre the slide, move the cursor to the azimuth on
TA or TB, set the index of C to the cursor and under
cos Lat on S and read the error on D.

Example—Lat 25°, Azimuth 57°.

Centre the slide, move the cursor to 57° on TB, set the

index of C to the cursor, move the cursor to cos 25° on S and read 1·395 on D.

Error = 1·395′.

Alternative setting:

Using $\dfrac{1}{\text{Error}} = \dfrac{1}{\tan \text{Az} \cos \text{Lat}}$

Set the Azimuth on TA or TB over the index of D, move the cursor to the index of C and set cos Lat on S to the cursor, then over the index of D read the error on C.

In the above example.

Set 57 on TB over the index of D, move the cursor to the index of C and set cos 25 to the cursor, then over the index of D read 1·395 on D.

Error 1·395′.

To find the Error in Longitude due to an Error of 1′ of Altitude.

Error = cosec Az, sec Lat.

Set sin Az on S over the index of D, move the cursor to the index of C and set cos Lat on S to the cursor, then under the index of C read the error on D.

Example—Lat 33°, Azimuth 39°.

Set sin 39 on S over the index of D, move the cursor to the index of C and set 33° on TA to the cursor, then under the index of C read 1·9 on D.

Error 1·9′.

To find the Error in the calculated Altitude due to an Error in the chosen Latitude.

Error = D. Lat, cos Azimuth.

Example—Using chosen Latitude 52° 00′ N., the calculated altitude was 41° 30′, Azimuth 055° T. = N. 55° E.

Find the calculated altitude for Latitude 52° 14′ N.

Set the index of C to 14 on D, move the cursor to cos 55 on S, and read 8·03 on D.

Calculated Alt.	=	41° 30′
Correction	=	8·03′
New Calculated Alt.	=	41° 21·97′

Latitude and Azimuth same name subtract.
Latitude and Azimuth opposite names add.

To find the Dip of the Shore Horizon.

$$\text{Dip} = \frac{h}{d} \times \cdot 565$$

Where Dip is in minutes

  h   is the height of eye in feet.
  d   is the distance in nautical miles.

Set d on C over h on D, then under ·565 on C read the Dip on D.

Example—Height of eye 42 ft. Distance of Shore horizon 1·4 nm.

Set 1·4 on C over 42 on D, move the cursor to the index of C, set the right index of C to the cursor, and under ·565 on C read 16·95 on D.

Alternatively use A and B scales to avoid resetting the slide or

Set 1·4 on C over 42 on D, move the cursor to the

index of C. Set ·565 on C1 to the cursor and under the index of C read 16·95 on D.

Dip = 16·95′.

To find the Dip of the Sea Horizon.

Dip = 0·984. $\sqrt{\text{Height of eye in ft.}}$

Set the index of B to the height of eye on A, then under ·984 on C read the Dip on D.

Example—Height of eye = 58 ft.

Set the index of B to 58 on A, and under ·984 on C read 7·5 on D.

Dip for 58 ft. = 7·5′.

To find the Parallax in Altitude.

Par in Alt = Horizontal Par . cos Alt.

Set the index of C to the Hor. Par. on D, move the cursor to cos Alt on S and read Par. in Alt on D.

Example—Hor. Par. = 54·2′, Alt = 42° 20′.

Set the index of C to 54·2 on D, move the cursor to cos 42° 20′ on S and read 40·1 on D.

Parallax in Altitude = 40·1′.

To find the Mean Refraction (Suitable for Altitudes above 10°).

Mean Refraction = ·94 cot Alt.

Set the altitude on TA or TB over ·94 on D and under the index of C read the Refraction on D.

Example—Altitude 20° 20'.

Set 20° 20' on TA over ·94 on D, and under the index of C read 2·54' on D.

Mean Refraction = 2·54'.

Example—Altitude 68° 40'.

Set 68° 40' on TB over ·94 on D and under the index of C read 0·37 on D.

Mean Refraction = 0·37'.

Ex Meridian Problems

To find the Reduction to the Meridian.

1st Method:

Reduction = ·5235 . cos Lat cos Dec sec Alt × HA². At ·5235 on D is a mark 'XM'.

Set the index of C to 'XM' on D, move the cursor to cos Lat on S, set cos Alt on S to the cursor, move the cursor to cos Dec on S, and under the cursor read 'X' on D.

Now set the index of C to the HA on D, and over 'X' on B, read the reduction on A.

Example—Lat 34° N., Dec 15° S., Alt 40° 30', Hour Angle 6° 18' (E).

Set the index of C to 'XM' on D, move the cursor cos 34 on S, set cos 40° 30' on S to the cursor, move the cursor to cos 15° on S and read ·551 on D.

Set the index of C to 6·3 (6° 18') on D and over ·551 on B read 21·9 on A.

Reduction 21·9'.

Using the setting for finding the azimuth gives azimuth S 8 E. and therefore P/L N82 E.—S 82 W.

2nd Method:

From the Table extract K for the Latitude and for the Declination interpolating as necessary.

> Same Name   Subtract
> Opposite Name   Add
> Then reduction $= \dfrac{HA^2}{K}$

Set the cursor to the HA on D and set K on B to the cursor, then over the index of B read the reduction on A.

Example—Lat 38° 30′ N., Dec 17° 15′ N., Hour Angle 5° 12′.

> K for Lat N 1·52
> K for Dec N ·59
> _____
> Subtract ·93

Set the cursor to 5·2° (5° 12′) on D, and set ·93 on B to the cursor, then over the index of B read 29·0 on A.

Reduction = 29·0′.

Example—Lat 13° 24′ N., Dec 35° 40′ S., Hour Angle 9° 27′.

> K for Lat N ·46
> K for Dec S 1·35
> _____
> Add 1·81

Set the index of C to 9·45 (9° 27′) on D, and set 1·81 on B to the cursor, then over the index of B read 49·5 on A.

Reduction = 49·5′.

EX-MERIDIAN TABLE

Lat. Dec.	K	Lat. Dec.	K	Lat. Dec.	K	Lat. Dec.	K
° ′		° ′		° ′		° ′	
0 30	0·02	20 30	0·72	40 30	1·63	60 30	3·38
1 00	0·03	21 00	0·73	41 00	1·66	61 00	3·45
1 30	0·05	21 30	0·75	41 30	1·69	61 30	3·52
2 00	0·07	22 00	0·77	42 00	1·72	62 00	3·59
2 30	0·08	22 30	0·79	42 30	1·75	62 30	3·69
3 00	0·10	23 00	0·81	43 00	1·78	63 00	3·75
3 30	0·12	23 30	0·83	43 30	1·81	63 30	3·83
4 00	0·13	24 00	0·85	44 00	1·84	64 00	3·92
4 30	0·15	24 30	0·87	44 30	1·89	64 30	4·01
5 00	0·17	25 00	0·89	45 00	1·91	65 00	4·10
5 30	0·18	25 30	0·91	45 30	1·94	65 30	4·19
6 00	0·20	26 00	0·93	46 00	1·98	66 00	4·29
6 30	0·22	26 30	0·95	46 30	2·01	66 30	4·40
7 00	0·23	27 00	0·97	47 00	2·05	67 00	4·50
7 30	0·25	27 30	1·00	47 30	2·08	67 30	4·61
8 00	0·27	28 00	1·02	48 00	2·12	68 00	4·73
8 30	0·29	28 30	1·04	48 30	2·16	68 30	4·85
9 00	0·30	29 00	1·06	49 00	2·20	69 00	4·97
9 30	0·32	29 30	1·08	49 30	2·24	69 30	5·10
10 00	0·34	30 00	1·10	50 00	2·28	70 00	5·24
10 30	0·35	30 30	1·13	50 30	2·32	70 30	5·39
11 00	0·37	31 00	1·15	51 00	2·36	71 00	5·55
11 30	0·39	31 30	1·17	51 30	2·40	71 30	5·71
12 00	0·41	32 00	1·19	52 00	2·44	72 00	5·88
12 30	0·42	32 30	1·22	52 30	2·49	72 30	6·06
13 00	0·44	33 00	1·24	53 00	2·53	73 00	6·25
13 30	0·46	33 30	1·26	53 30	2·58	73 30	6·45
14 00	0·48	34 00	1·29	54 00	2·63	74 00	6·66
14 30	0·49	34 30	1·31	54 30	2·68	74 30	6·88
15 00	0·51	35 00	1·34	55 00	2·73	75 00	7·13
15 30	0·53	35 30	1·36	55 30	2·78	75 30	7·39
16 00	0·55	36 00	1·39	56 00	2·83	76 00	7·66
16 30	0·57	36 30	1·42	56 30	2·88	76 30	7·96
17 00	0·58	37 00	1·44	57 00	2·94	77 00	8·28
17 30	0·60	37 30	1·47	57 30	3·00	77 30	8·60
18 00	0·62	38 00	1·49	58 00	3·06	78 00	8·99
18 30	0·64	38 30	1·52	58 30	3·12	78 30	9·40
19 00	0·66	39 00	1·55	59 00	3·18	79 00	9·83
19 30	0·68	39 30	1·57	59 30	3·24	79 30	10·31
20 00	0·70	40 00	1·60	60 00	3·31	80 00	10·83

Great Circle Sailing

To find the Distance and Initial and Final Courses.

Haversine $\theta = \sin^2 \dfrac{\theta}{2}$

Use the haversine formula making this substitution.

To find the Distance.

Hav AB = hav P sin PA sin PB+hav (PA∼PB).

$$\text{Sin}^2 \frac{AB}{2} = \sin^2 \frac{P}{2} \sin PA \sin PB + \sin^2 \frac{PA∼PB}{2}$$

To find the Initial and Final Courses.

Having found the distance, use may be made of the sine formula.

Sin A = sin P.cosec AB.sin PB.

Sin B = sin P.cosec AB.sin PA.

The settings for this problem will best be shewn by an example.

Example—To find the Great Circle Distance and the Initial and Final Courses from A (27° 40′ N., 152° 08′ E.) to B (55° 28′ N., 149° 20′ W.)

P (D. Long) 58° 32′ $\dfrac{P}{2} = 29° 16′$

PA (Co—Lat A) 62° 20′   PA∼PB = 27° 48′

PB (Co—Lat B) 34° 32′ $\dfrac{PA−PB}{2} = 13° 54′$

$\text{Sin}^2 \dfrac{AB}{2} = \sin^2 29° 16′$. Sin 62° 20′. Sin 34° 32′+ $\sin^2$ 13° 54′.

Set the cursor to sin 29° 16′ on S, and read ·239 on B.
Hav 58° 32′ = 0·239.

Set the index of C to ·239 on D, move the cursor to
sin 62° 20′ on S, set the index of C to the cursor, move
the cursor to sin 34° 32′ on S and read ·120 on D.

Set the cursor to sin 13° 54′ on S, and read ·058 on B.
0·120+0·058 = 0·178.

Set the cursor to 0·178 on B and read 24° 57′ on the
sine scale of S.

$$\frac{AB}{2} = 24° 57′. \qquad AB = 49° 54′.$$

Distance = 49° 54′.   2994 nm.

To find the Initial and Final Courses.

Sin A = sin 58° 32′ . cosec 49° 54′ . sin 34° 32′.
Sin B = sin 58° 32′ . cosec 49° 54′ . sin 62° 20′.

Set sin 58° 32′ on S to the index of D, move the
cursor to sin 49° 54′ on S, set sin 34° 32′ on S to the
cursor, move the cursor to the index of D and read
39° 15′ on the sine scale of S.

A = 39° 15′.

Set sin 58° 32′ on S to the index of D, move the
cursor to sin 49° 54′ on S, set sin 62° 20′ on S to the
cursor, move the cursor to the index of D and read 81°
on the sine scale of S.

B = 81° 00′

Distance 2994 nm.
Initial Course 039° 15′.
Final Course 081° 00′.

F

These results compare well with those obtained by working the problem in full by logarithms.

The calculated answers being:

2992 nm., 039° 12′, and 080° 58′.

CHAPTER VII

COASTAL NAVIGATION

To find the Distance to the Visible Horizon.

Distance $= 1.15 \times \sqrt{\text{Height in ft.}}$

Set the index of B to height in feet on A, and under 1·15 on C read the distance in miles on D.

Example—Height of eye 42 ft.

Set the index of B to 42 on A and under 1·15 on C read 7·45 on D.

Distance $= 7.45$ nm.

Example—Height of light 150 ft., height of eye 38 ft.

To find the range of the light.

Set the index of B to 150 on A, and under 1·15 on C read 14·1 in D.

Set the index of B to 38 on A, and under 1·15 on C read 7·1 on D.

Range $= 14.1 + 7.1 = 21.2$ nm.

Example—Range of light given on chart as 17', height of eye 33 ft.

Set the index of B to 15 on A and under 1·15 on C read 4·45 on D.

Set the index of B to 33 on A, and under 1·15 on C read 6·6 on D.

Range $= 17 - 4.45 + 6.6 = 19.15$ nm.

Given Range and Bearing. To find the distance a vessel will pass abeam, and the distance to run to the beam bearing.

Distance off abeam = Range . sin Relative Bearing.
Distance to run   = Range . cos Relative Bearing.

Example—A vessel observed a light distant 18′, bearing 38° on the bow.

Set the index of C to 18 on D, move the cursor to sin 38 on S and read 11·1 on D, move the cursor to cos 38 and read 14·2 on D.

> Distance off Abeam = 11·1 nm.
> Distance to Run   = 14·2 nm.

Given Range and Bearing. To find the course to steer to pass a given distance off abeam, and the distance to run.

$$\text{Sin Relative Bearing} = \frac{\text{Distance off abeam}}{\text{Range}}$$

Distance to run   = Range . cos Relative Bearing.

Example—A light was observed bearing 112° T, distant 17′. Find course to steer to pass the light 5′ to Port, and the distance to run to bring it abeam.

Set the index of C to 17 on D, move the cursor to 5 on D, and under the cursor read sin 17° on S.

Set the index of C to 17 (miles) on D, move the cursor to cos 17° on S and read 16·25 on D.

> Bearing of Light 112° T
> Relative Bearing   17°
> _____
> Course to Steer   129° T

N.B.—To pass to Port add the Relative Bearing and to pass to Starboard subtract it.

> Distance to run = 16·25′.

To find the Distance off by two Bearings and the run between.

Set the cursor to the difference of the two bearings on S1, and set the Distance Run on B to the cursor. Move the cursor to the first angle on the bow on S1, and read the distance off at the second bearing on B, move the cursor to the second angle on the bow on S1 and read the distance off at the first bearing on B.

Example—A vessel observed a light bearing 25° on the bow, and after running 9 miles it bore 64° on the bow.

Set the cursor to 39° (64°−25°) on S1 and set 9 on B to the cursor. Move the cursor 25° on S1 and read 6·05 on B, move the cursor to 64° on S1 and read 12·85 on D.

Distance off at first bearing　　= 12·85′

Distance off at second bearing　= 6·05′

To find the distance off abeam by a single bearing and the run to the beam bearing.

Distance off = Distance run × tan Angle on the Bow.

Set the index of C to the distance run on D, move the cursor to the angle on the bow on TA or TB and read the distance off abeam on D.

Example—A light was observed 31° on the bow and after running for 7·5 miles it was abeam.

Set the index of C to 7·5 on D, move the cursor to 31° on TA and read 4·5 on D.

Distance off abeam = 4·5 ml.

Example—A light was observed 54° on the bow, and after running for 5·2 ml. it was abeam.

Set the index of C to 5·2 on D, move the cursor to 54° on TB and read 7·15 on D.

Distance off abeam = 7·15 ml.

To find Angles on the Bow such that the distance run is equal to the distance off when abeam.

Cot θ^2 = cot θ^1-1.

Where θ^1 is the first angle on the Bow and θ^2 is the second angle on the Bow.

Example—A light bore 30° on the bow, to what bearing must it be brought for the distance run to be equal to the distance off a beam?

Set the cursor to the index of D and set 30° on TA to the cursor, then under the index of C read 1·735 (cot 30°) on D.

Now set the index of C to 0·735 (1·735−1) on D, set the cursor to the index of D and read 54° on TB.

Second Angle on the Bow = 54°.

To find $\frac{1}{2}$ Convergency or Conversion Angle.

This is the correction to apply to a Radio Bearing to convert it to a Rhumb-line bearing.

Conversion Angle = $\frac{1}{2}$ D. Long. Sin Mean Lat.

Set the index of C to the $\frac{1}{2}$ D. Long on D, move the cursor to sin Mean Lat on S and read the Conversion Angle on D.

or

Set 2 on C over the D. Long on D, move the cursor to sin Mean Lat on S and read the Conversion Angle on D.

Example—D. Long 4° 30′. Mean Lat 47° 30′.

Set 2 on C over 4·5 (4° 30′) on D, move the cursor to sin 47° 30′ on S, and read 1·66 on D.

or

Set the index of C to 2·25 on D, move the cursor to sin 47° 30′ on S and read 1·66.

Conversion Angle = 1·66° = 1° 40′.

Vertical Danger Angle.

$$\theta = \frac{h \times \cdot565}{d}$$

Where θ' = Danger Angle in minutes of arc.

h = Height in feet.

d = Distance in miles.

Set d on C to h on D and under $\cdot565$ on C read the Danger Angle in minutes on D.

Example—Height 175 ft.   Distance 2′.

Set 2 on C over 175 on D and under $\cdot565$ on C read 49·5 on D.

Danger Angle = 49·5′.

To find the distance off by Vertical Angle. Object not beyond the Visible Horizon.

$$d = \frac{h \times \cdot565}{\theta'}$$

Where d = Distance off in miles.

h = Height in feet.

θ' = Vertical Angle in minutes of arc.

Set θ on C over h on D and under $\cdot565$ on C read d on D.

Example—Height 112 ft.   Vertical Angle 1° 22′ (82′).

Set 82 on C over 112 on D and under $\cdot565$ on C read $\cdot77$ on D.

Distance off 0·77 ml.

Note that here having set 82 on C over 112 on D, it was necessary to move the cursor to the right index of C, and set the left index of C to the cursor before reading $\cdot565$ on C. At any time the A and B scales may be used instead of C and D, when this resetting of the slide becomes unnecessary but a certain amount of accuracy is lost.

To find the distance off by Vertical Angle. Object beyond the Visible Horizon.

Correct the Sextant Reading for Dip and Refraction. To do this, from the observed altitude subtract the Dip for the Height of Eye and also 1/12 of the estimated distance.

Allow for curvature of the earth by subtracting from the height of the object, in feet, $0.9 \times$ square of the estimated distance in miles. Then proceed as before.

$$d = \frac{h \times \cdot 565}{\theta'}$$

Example—The observed altitude of a hill, approximately 30 miles distant, Height 5820 ft., was 1° 44′, the Height of Eye being 32 ft.

Obs Alt	=	1° 44′
Dip = ·984 $\sqrt{h}$ =		−5·6
1/12 × 30	=	−2·5
Correct Alt	=	1° 35·9′ = 95·9′

Set the index of C to 30 (miles) on D and over ·9 on B read 810 on A.

Height	5820 ft.
Correction for Curvature	−810 ft.
Corrected height	5010 ft.

Set 95·9 on C over 5010 on D and under ·565 on C, read 29·5 on D.

Distance off = 29·5 ml.

To find the Course to steer and speed made good counteracting a current.

Course-Current Angle = Angular difference between the course and the direction of the current.

Set the cursor to the course-current angle on S1, and set the steaming speed on B to the cursor. Move the cursor to the rate of the current on B, and read the drift angle on S1. Set the cursor to course-current angle plus drift angle on S1, and read the speed made good on B.

When finding the course-current angle. If the course is greater than the current direction add the drift angle to the course to find the course to steer and if less than the current direction subtract it.

i.e. Port Drift+, Starboard Drift−.

Example—A vessel wishes to make good a course of 058°, through a current setting 104° at 2 knots. Steaming speed 18·5 knots.

Set the cursor to 46° (104−58) on S1, and set 18·5 on B to the cursor. Move the cursor to 2 on B and read $4\frac{1}{2}$° on S1. Set the cursor to $50\frac{1}{2}$° ($46+4\frac{1}{2}$) on S1 and read 19·8 on D.

Course to steer = $058-4\frac{1}{2} = 053\frac{1}{2}$°.
Speed made good = 19·8 knots.

Example—To make good a course of 037° T, through a current setting 254° at 3 knots, steaming speed 17·4 knots.

Course-current angle = 037−254 = 397−254 = 143°.

Set the cursor to 143° on S1 and set 17·4 on B to the cursor, move the cursor to 3 on B and read 6° on S1. Move the cursor to 149° (143+6) on S1 and read 14·85 on D.

Star. Drift.   Course = 037−6 = 031° T.
                 Speed made good = 14·85 knots.

To find the distance to run to bring a light to a given bearing, and the distance off at that bearing.

Set the cursor to the required angle on the bow on S1 and set the original distance off on B to the cursor, then move the cursor to the original angle on the bow on S1 and read the distance off on B, and move the cursor to the difference between the bearings on S1 and read the distance to run on B.

Example—A light bore 18° on the bow, distant 14 miles. Find the distance to run to bring it 50° on the bow and the distance off at that bearing.

Set the cursor to 50° on S1 and set 14 on B to the cursor. Move the cursor to 18° on S1 and read 5·65 on B. Move the cursor to 32° (50—18) on S1 and read 9·7 on B.

> Distance to run = 9·7 ml.
> Distance off   = 5·65 ml.

Reduction to Soundings

See accompanying figure

To find the correction to the Lead Line.

$$\text{Correction to L.W. (H.W.)} = \tfrac{1}{2} \text{ range} - \tfrac{1}{2} \text{ range, cos } \theta.$$
$$= \tfrac{1}{2} \text{ range } (1 - \cos \theta).$$
$$= \tfrac{1}{2} \text{ range, versine } \theta.$$
$$= \text{Range . hav } \theta.$$
$$= \text{Range . sin}^2 . \frac{\theta}{2}$$

This is the form of the formula best used on the Slide Rule.

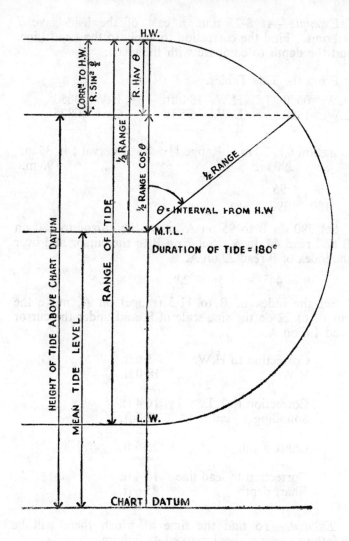

Example—At 8-25 a.m. a cast of the lead gave 7 fathoms. Find the correction to apply to the Lead Line, and the depth to compare with the chart.

From the Tide Tables.

| H.W. | 0650 | H.W. | 18·0 ft. | H.W. | 0650 |
| L.W. | 1320 | L.W. | 6·5 ft. | Cast | 0825 |

Duration 6 h. 30 m.　Range 11·5 ft.　Interval 1 h. 35 m.
　　,,　　　390 m.　　　　　　　　　　　　　,,　　　　95 m.

$$\frac{\theta}{180} = \frac{95}{390}$$

Set 390 on B to 95 on A, move the cursor to 180 on B and read 44 on A. Set 2 on B to the cursor and over the index of B read 22 on A.

$$\theta = 44° \qquad \tfrac{1}{2}\theta = 22°.$$

Set the index of B to 11·5 (range) on A, move the cursor to 22 on the sine scale of S, and under the cursor read 1·6 on A.

Correction to H.W.	1·6 ft.
H.W.	18·0 ft.
Correction to L.L.	16·4 ft.
Sounding	42·0 ft.
Chart depth	25·6 ft.
Correction to lead line	16·4 ft.
Chart depth	25·6 ft.

Example—To find the time at which there will be 6 fathoms over a shoal marked $4\tfrac{1}{2}$ fathoms.

From the Tide Tables:

L.W. 0240	L.W.	3·3 ft.	Req'd Depth 36·0 ft.	L.W.	3·3 ft.
H.W. 0824	H.W.	12·8 ft.	Chart Depth 27·0 ft.	Corr to L.L.	9·0 ft.
Dur. 5·44	Range	9·5 ft.	Corr to L.L. 9·0 ft.	,, L.W.	5·7 ft.
344m.					

Set the index of B to 9·5 (range) on A and move the cursor to 5·7 on A. Then under the cursor read 50° 45′ on the sine scale of S.

$$\frac{\theta}{2} = 50° 45'. \qquad\qquad \theta = 101·5°.$$

Set 180 on B to 101·5 on A, then over 344 on B read 194 on A.

Interval from L.W. 194 min. or 3 hr. 14 min.

L.W.	0240
Interval	0314
Req'd Time	0554

At 0554 hrs. there will be 6 fathoms over a patch marked 4½ fathoms.

CHAPTER VIII

AIR NAVIGATION

Special Settings and Scales

ALL airmen are familiar with the Appleyard Scale on the Navigational Computor. This scale is, of course, a simple type of slide rule, accurate enough for rough calculations, such as are required in flight. However, for flight planning and in the examination room a higher degree of accuracy is called for, and this must be obtained with the minimum of delay. It is here that the Slide Rule, properly handled, is absolutely invaluable. Any calculations normally made on the computor, in flight planning, can be made quicker and more accurately on the slide rule.

Special Settings.

Use as a Navigational Computer to find the Course and Ground Speed given T.A.S., Track, and Wind Velocity.

Use Scales S1 and B on the face of the rule.

NOTE—Wind-track angle is the difference between the wind and track directions.

Set the cursor to the wind-track angle on S1 and set the T.A.S. on B to the cursor.

Move the cursor to the wind-speed on B and under the cursor read the drift on S1.

Now move the cursor to the wind-track angle minus drift on S1 and under the cursor read the ground-speed on B.

Example—Given: Track 110° T, T.A.S. 185 knots. W.V. 075°/40 knots.

∴Wind-track angle = 35° (110—75)

Set the cursor to 35° on S1 and set 185 on B to the cursor. Move the cursor to 40 on B and read 7° on S1, Now move the cursor to 28 (35—7) on S1 and read 151 on B.

Course   = 103° T (110—7)

Ground Speed = 151 knots.

Note that when finding the wind-track angle, if the wind direction is subtracted from the track, the drift is to starboard, but if the track has to be subtracted from the wind direction, the drift is to port.

Course = Track—Star drift.

or   Track+Port drift.

Example—Given: Track 200° T, T.A.S. 210 knots, W.V. 330/45 knots. Wind-track angle = 130° (330—200).

Set the cursor to 130 on S1 and set 210 on B to the cursor. Move the cursor to 45 on B and read 9½° on S1. Now move the cursor to 120½ (130—9½) on S1 and read 236 on B.

Course = 209½ T (200+9½).

Ground Speed = 236 knots.

Conversion of Feet to Metres.

On the face of the rule are marked certain gauge points: M for metres, FT for feet, KG for Kilograms, LB for pounds, IMP for Imperial gallons, U.S.G. for U.S. Gallons and LIT for Litres.

Set the cursor to FT and then set any number of feet on B to the cursor. Move the cursor to M and under the cursor read the equivalent in Metres.

Example—To convert 55 ft. to metres.

Set the cursor to FT and set 55 on B to the cursor. Move the cursor to M and read 16·8 on B.

$$55 \text{ ft.} = 16·8 \text{ m.}$$

Example—To convert 9 m. to feet.

Set the cursor to M and set 9 on B to the cursor. Move the cursor to FT and read 29·5 on B.

$$9 \text{ m} = 29·5 \text{ ft.}$$

Conversion of lbs. to kg.

Set the cursor to LB and set any number of lbs. on B to the cursor, move the cursor to KG and under the cursor read the equivalent in kg.

Example—To convert 70 lb. to kg.

Set the cursor to LB and set 70 on B to the cursor. Move the cursor to KG and read 31·8 on B.

$$70 \text{ lb.} = 31·8 \text{ kg.}$$

Example—To convert 180 kg. to lbs.

Set the cursor to KG and set 180 on B to the cursor, move the cursor to LB and read 396 on B.

$$180 \text{ kg.} = 396 \text{ lb.}$$

Conversion of Imperial Gallons, U.S. Gallons and Litres.

These are worked exactly the same as converting feet to metres and lbs. to kg.

Example—To convert 25 Imp. Gall. to U.S. Gall. and Litres.

Set the cursor to IMP and set 25 on B to the cursor. Move the cursor to U.S. Gall. and read 30 on B. Move the cursor to LIT and read 113·5 on B.

25 Imp. Gall. = 30 U.S. Gall. = 113·5 litres.

Example—To convert 90 litres to gallons.

Set the cursor to LIT and set 90 on B to the cursor. Move the cursor to IMP and read 19·8. Move the cursor to U.S.G. and read 23·8 on B.

90 litres = 19·8 Imp. Gall. = 23·8 U.S. Gall.

Flight Planning.

To convert A.M.P.G. to G.P.H.

$$\text{G.P.H.} = \frac{\text{T.A.S.}}{\text{A.M.P.G.}}$$

Set the A.M.P.G. on C over the T.A.S. on D and under the index of C read the G.P.H. on D.

Example—T.A.S. 240 knots. Air Nautical Miles per gallon 1·25.

Set 1·25 on C over 240 on D and under the index of C read 192 on D.

$$\text{G.P.H.} = 192.$$

When the A.M.P.G. is in statute miles and the T.A.S. is given in knots. Set the A.M.P.G. on C over the T.A.S. on D. Move the cursor to the index of C and read the G.P.H. on S.M.

Example—T.A.S. 250 knots. A.M.P.G. (statute) 1·12.

Set 1·12 on the C over 250 on D, move the cursor to the index of C and read 257 on S.M.

$$\text{G.P.H.} = 257.$$

G

To convert G.P.H. to A.M.P.G.

$$A.M.P.G. = \frac{T.A.S.}{G.P.H.}$$

Set the G.P.H. on C over the T.A.S. on D and under the index of C read the A.M.P.G. on D.

Example—T.A.S. 212 knots. G.P.H. 224.

Set 224 on C over 212 on D and under the index of C read ·946 on D.

$$A.M.P.G. = ·946.$$

To convert G.M.P.G. to G.P.H., etc.

Similarly to the above.

$$G.P.H. = \frac{G./S.}{G.M.P.G.} \quad \text{and} \quad G.M.P.G. = \frac{G./S.}{G.P.H.}$$

Example—G./S. 224 knots. G.P.H. 192.

Set 192 on C over 224 on D and under the index of C read 1·165 on D.

$$G.M.P.G. = 1·165.$$

To convert A.M.P.G. to G.M.P.G.

$$\frac{T.A.S.}{A.M.P.G.} = \frac{G./S.}{G.M.P.G.}$$

Set A.M.P.G. on C over T.A.S. on D, then over G./S. on D read the G.M.P.G. on C.

Example—T.A.S. 222 knots. G./S. 246 knots A.M.P.G. 1·2.

Set 1·2 on C over 222 on D and over 246 on D read 1·33 on C.

$$G.M.P.G. = 1·33.$$

To find Total Time and Consumption.

Given G./S., G.P.H. and Total Distance.

$$\text{Time} = \frac{\text{Distance}}{\text{G./S.}} \qquad \text{Consumption} = \text{Time} \times \text{G.P.H.}$$

Set G./S. on C over Total Distance on D, and under the index of C read the Time in hours on D, or move the cursor to 60 on C and read the Time in minutes on D. Now move the cursor to the G.P.H. on C and read the Consumption on D.

Example—G./S. 218 knots, G.P.H. 242, Distance 1220 miles.

Set 218 on C over 1220 on D and under the index of C read 5·6 on D, move the cursor to 60 on C and read 336 on D. Now move the cursor to 242 on C and read 1354 on D.

Time taken 5·6 hours = 336 min.

Consumption 1354 gall.

To find the Maximum Range in Time and Distance.

Given Av. G./S., G.P.H., and Fuel available.

$$\text{Time} = \frac{\text{Fuel available}}{\text{G.P.H.}} \qquad \text{Distance} = \text{Time} \times \text{G./S.}$$

Set G.P.H. on C over Fuel available on D, then under the index of C read the time in hours on D, and under 60 on C the time in minutes on D and under the G./S. on C read the Distance on D.

Example—Av. G./S. 218 knots. Av. G.P.H. 242 Gall., Fuel available 2740 gall.

Set 242 on C over 2740 on D, then under the index of C read 11·33 (hours) on D, under 60 on C read 680 (mins.) on D, and under 218 on C read 2470 on D.

Maximum Time 11·33 hours = 680 min.

Maximum Distance 2470 ml.

To find the Critical Point.

$$\text{Distance to C.P.} = \frac{\text{Total Distance} \times \text{G./S. home}}{\text{G./S. out} + \text{G./S. home}}$$

Set (G./S. out+G./S. home) on C, over G./S. home on D then under the Total Distance on C read the distance to the C.P. on D.

Example—Total Distance 420 miles, G./S. out 175 knots, G./S. home 210 knots.

Set 385 (175+210) on C over 210 on D, then under 420 on C read 229 on D.

Distance to C.P. = 229 ml.

To find the Point of No Return.

$$\text{Time out to P.N.R.} = \frac{\text{Endurance} \times \text{G./S. home}}{\text{G./S. out} + \text{G./S. home}}$$

Set (G./S. out+G./S. home) on C over G./S. home on D, and under the Endurance on C read the Time to P.N.R. on D.

Example—Endurance 4 hr. (240 min.) G./S. out 220 knots, G./S. home 194 knots.

Set 414 (220+194) on C over 194 on D, and under 240 on C read 112½ on D.

Time to P.N.R. 112½ min. = 1 hr. 52½ min.

Point of No Return with Variable Fuel Flow.

$$\text{Distance to P.N.R.} = \frac{\text{Fuel Available}}{\dfrac{\text{Fuel Flow}}{\text{G./S.}}\text{out} + \dfrac{\text{Fuel Flow}}{\text{G./S.}}\text{home}}$$

Example—Fuel available 25,000 kg.
G./S. out 420 Knots, Fuel Flow out 6400 Kg./Hr.
G./S. home 465 knots, Fuel Flow home 5800 Kg./Hr.

Set 420 on C to 6400 on D. Under index of C read 15·25 on D.

Set 465 on C to 5800 on D. Under index of C read 12·45 on D.

$$\text{Distance} = \frac{25000}{15·25+12·45} = \frac{25000}{27·7} = 902 \text{ ml.}$$

Distance to P.N.R. 902 miles.

To find the Time to Reach the P.N.R.

902 ml. at 420 knots.

Set 60 on C to 420 on D, and under 902 on DF read 129 min. on CF.

Time taken 129 min. = 2 hr. 9 min.

Pressure Pattern Flying.

Single Heading Flight.

$$Zn = \frac{21·47 \; (H_1 \sim H_0)}{\text{T.A.S.} \times \sin \theta}$$

Example—Heights: Departing 18,200 ft. Arriving 17,400 ft.

T.A.S. 220 knots, Mean Lat. 52° N.

Set 220 on C over 21·47 on D, move the cursor to 800 (18,200−17,400) on C, set sin 52° on S to the cursor and under the index of C read 99 on D.

Zn = 99 ml.

$$Vn = \frac{21·47 \; (H_1 \sim H_0)}{\text{Air Dist.} \times \sin \theta}$$

Example—Heights: Departing 15,400, Arriving 16,000.

Air Distance 700 ml., Lat 48° N.

Set 700 on C over 21·47 on D, move the cursor to 600 (16,000—15,400) on C, set sin 48° on S to the cursor, and under the index of C read 24·8 on D.

Vn = 24·8 knots.

$$\text{Sin Drift} = \frac{21·47 \, (H_1 \sim H_0)}{\text{Dist. sin } \theta \times \text{T.A.S.}}$$

Example—Difference of Height 790 ft., Distance 890 ml.

T.A.S. 242 knots, Mean Lat 50° 30′ N.

Set 242 on C over 21·47 on D, move the cursor to 790 on C and set 890 on C to the cursor, move the cursor to the index of C and set sin 50° 30′ on S to the cursor. Move the cursor to the index of C, centre the slide, and read, under the cursor, sin 5° 52′ on S.

Drift = 5° 52′.

N.B.—In flight the Difference of Altimeter Errors should be used for $H_1 \sim H_0$.

If the heights are given in metres instead of feet, use the figure 70·42 in place of 21·47.

Chart Scales.

Mercator Charts.

Scale varies as Sec. Latitude.

Example—If the scale of a Mercator Chart is 1/1,000,000 in Lat 56° N., find the scale at the Equator, the scale in Lat 40° N., and also in what latitude the scale will be $\dfrac{1}{1,450,000}$

Set the cursor to 1,000,000 (the index) of D and set the Latitude on the cosine scale of S to the cursor. Then under any Latitude on the cos scale read the scale in that latitude on the D scale.

Under 0 (the index) of the cos scale read 1,791,000 on D.

Scale of Equator = 1/1,791,000.

Under 40 on the cos scale read 1,371,000 on D.
Scale at 40° N. = 1/1,371,000.

Over 1,450,000 on D read 36° on the cos scale.
Scale 1/1,450,000 in Lat 36°.

Example—Scale of Chart 1/2,500,000 at 50° N.

Find the scale at the Equator, and the length of 1 meridional part.

Set cos 50° on S over 2,500,000 on D. Under the index of C read 3,890,000 on D.

Scale at Equator = 1/3,890,000.

Length of a mer. part 72,960 × Scale inches.

Set 72,960 on C over 3,890,000 on D and over the index of D read ·01875 on C.

1 mer. part = ·01875 in.

N.B.—72,960 = 6080 × 12 inches in a nautical mile.

Polar Stereographic Charts.

Scale varies as $\text{Sec}^2 . \frac{1}{2}$ Colat.

Example—Given the scale at the Pole is 1/4,000,000. To find the scale in Lat 70° N.

Set the index of B to 4,000,000 on A, move the cursor to cos 10 $\left(\dfrac{90-70}{2}\right)$ on S, and read 3,880,000 on A.

Scale at 70° N. = 1/3,880,000.

Example—Given the scale at 70° N. is 1/1,250,000. To find the scale at the Pole, and at 60° N.

Set the cursor to 1,250,000 on A. Set $\cos 10 \left(\dfrac{90-70}{2}\right)$ on S to the cursor, then over the index of B, read 1,285,000 on A, and over $\cos 15 \left(\dfrac{90-60}{2}\right)$ on S read 1,200,000 on A.

Scale at the Pole = 1/1,285,000.

Scale at 60° N. = 1/1,200,000

Mach Meter Settings.

To find the Speed of Sound.

Speed of Sound = $38 \cdot 94 \times \sqrt{\text{Temperature (Abs)}}$

Example—To find the speed of sound at −43° C.
−43° C = 273°−43° = 230° A.

Set the index of B to 230 on A, move the cursor to 38·94 on C and read 592 on D.

Speed of Sound = 592 knots.

To find the Mach No.

$$M = \frac{\text{T.A.S.}}{\text{Sp. of Sd.}}$$

Example—To find the Mach No. flying at 430 knots at −48° C.

−48° C. = 273°−48° = 225° A.

Set the index of B to 225 on A, move the cursor to 38·94 on C, set 430 on C to the cursor and over the index of D read ·735 on C.

Mach No. = ·735.

To find the T.A.S.

T.A.S. $= M \times$ Speed of Sound.

Example—To find the T.A.S. flying at Mach 0·8 at $-38°$ C.

$$-38° \text{ C} = 273° - 38° = 235° \text{ A.}$$

Set the index of B to 235 on A, move the cursor to 38·94 on C, set the index of C to the cursor and under 0·8 on C read 478 on D.

T.A.S. $= 478$ knots.

To find the Temperature.

$$\sqrt{\text{Temp}} \text{ (A)} = \frac{\text{Sp. of Sd.}}{38·94} = \frac{\text{T.A.S.}}{M \times 38·94}$$

Example—To find the Temperature at which the T.A.S. would be 460 knots at Mach 0·76.

Set ·76 on C to 460 on D, move the cursor to the index of C and read 605 on D. Set 38·94 on C to the cursor and over the index of B read 241 on A.

Speed of Sound $= 605$ knots.

Temperature $= 241°$ A. $= -32°$ C.

CHAPTER IX

MISCELLANEOUS PROBLEMS

Meteorology

Difference of Height per m.b.

$$H \text{ (feet)} = \frac{96 \cdot T}{P}. \quad H \text{ (metres)} = \frac{29 \cdot 27 \cdot T}{P}$$

Where H is the difference of height.

T is the Mean Temperature in Absolute.

P is the Mean Pressure in milibars.

Example—To find the difference of height in feet between 995 mb with Temperature 282° A. and 970 mb with Temperature 280° A.

Mean Pressure 982·5 m.b.   Mean Temperature 281° A.
Change of Pressure 25 m.b.

$$H = \frac{96 \cdot T}{P} \times 25$$

Set the index of C to 96 on D, move the cursor to 281 on C, set 982·5 on C to the cursor. Over 25 on CF read 686 ft. on DF.

$$\underline{\text{Thickness of layer} = 686 \text{ ft.}}$$

Example—To find the thickness of the layer, between 850 m.b. with Temp. 270° A. and 810 m.b. with Temp. 266° m.b., in metres.

Mean Press. 830 m.b.   Mean Temp. 268° A.
Change of Press. 40 m.b.

Set the index of C to 29·27 on D, move the cursor to 268 on CF, set 830 on CF to the cursor. Under 40 on C read 378 metres on D.

Thickness of layer = 378 metres.

Pressure—Height Formula.

H (feet) = $221·1 \times T$ (Log P_0 — Log P_1)
H (metres) = $67·4 \times T$ (Log P_0 — Log P_1)

Example—To find the Height of the 820 m.b. level, given that M.S.L. Pressure is 1010 m.b., and the Mean Temperature is $+7·5°$ C.

$+7·5$ C. = 280·5 A.

Set 820 on C over 1010 on D, move the cursor to the index of C and read ·090 on L.

∴ Log P_0 — Log P_1 = ·090.

Set the index of C to ·09 on D, move the cursor to 221·1 on C, set the index of C to the cursor and under 280·5 on C read 5580 on D.

Alternatively—

Set the cursor to ·09 on C and set 221·1 on C1 to the cursor, move the cursor to 280·5 on C and read 5580 on D.

Height = 5580 ft.

This problem could have been worked exactly as laid out in the formula, thus:

Set the cursor to 1010 on D and read 3·004 on L.
Set the cursor to 820 on D and read 2·914 on L.

Difference   ·090

and then proceed as before.

Example—To find the I.C.A.N. Pressure at 8000 ft.

M.S.L. Pressure 1013·2 m.b.
Mean Temperature $288 - 4 \times 1·98 = 280·08$ A.

$$\text{Log } P_1 = \text{Log } P_0 - \frac{H}{221·1 \times T}. \text{ (where H is in feet), } or$$

$$\text{Log } P_1 = \text{Log } P_0 - \frac{H}{67·4 \times T}. \text{ (where H is in meters).}$$

Set 221·1 on C to the index of D, move the cursor 8000 on C, set 280·08 on C to the cursor, and under the index of C read ·129 on D. Set the cursor to ·129 on L and 1013·2 on C to the cursor then over the index of D read 753 on C.

Pressure = 753 m.b.

A little explanation of this method is perhaps required

here. The formula $\text{Log } P_1 = \text{Log } P_0 - \frac{H}{221·1 \, T}$ may be

translated as $P_1 = P_0$ divided by the number whose log

is $\frac{H}{221·1 \, T}$.

It is this form that has been used in the above setting.

An alternative method would be—

Set 221·1 on C over the index of D, move the cursor to 8000 on D, and set 280·08 on C to the cursor, then under the index of C read ·129 on D.

Set the cursor to 1013·2 on D and read 3·006 on L
Subtract ·129

$$\therefore \text{Log } p_1 = \overline{2·877}$$

Set the cursor to ·877 on L and read 753 on D.
Pressure 753 m.b.

To find the Relative Density.

$$\rho = \frac{P}{R.T.}$$

$$\therefore \rho \propto \frac{P}{T}$$

The pressure at M.S.L. is 1013·2 m.b. and the temperature 288 A.

$$\therefore \text{The rel. dens.} = \frac{P_1}{T_1} \times \frac{T_0}{P_0}$$

To find the Relative Density where pressure is 750 m.b. and Temperature 280 A.

$$\text{Rel. Dens.} = \frac{750}{280} \times \frac{288}{1013 \cdot 2}$$

Set 280 on C over 750 on D, move the cursor to 288 on C, set 1013·2 on C to the cursor and under the index of C read ·760 on D.

$$\text{Relative Density} = \cdot 760.$$

Geostrophic Wind Formula.

$$V = \frac{G}{2 \omega \rho \sin \theta}$$

$$\therefore V \propto \frac{G}{\rho \sin \theta} \ or \ \frac{G}{\dfrac{P}{T} \sin \theta}$$

$\therefore$ For a constant gradient of pressure.

$$V \propto \frac{P \sin \theta}{T}$$

Example—Given a Geostrophic wind-scale for Lat 55, Temp. 15° C. and a pressure of 1010 m.b. To find the percentage correction when used in Lat 45, with pressure 1020 m.b. and Temp.+25° C.

15° C = 288° A, 25° C. = 298° A.

$$\frac{V_1}{V_0} = \frac{1010}{288} \times \frac{298}{1020} \times \frac{\sin 55}{\sin 45}$$

Set 288 on C over 1010 on D, move the cursor to 298 on C, set 1020 on C to the cursor, move the cursor to sin 55 on S, set sin 45 on S to the cursor and under the index of C read 1·186 on D.

Correction 18·6% to add.

Compass Calculations.

Devn. = A+B . sin co+C . cos co+D . sin 2 co+E. cos 2 co.

Each item must be worked separately.

Example—Given A = +2, B = −5, C = +4, D = +2, E = +1.

To find the deviation on 055° C.

∴ Devn. = +2+(−5) . sin 55+4 . cos 55+2 . sin 110 +(−1) . cos 110

= +2−5 . sin 55+4 . cos 55+2 . sin 70+1 . cos 70.

Set the index of C to 5 on D, move the cursor to sin 55 on S and read 4·1 on D.

Set the index of C to 4 on D, move the cursor to cos 55 on S and read 2·3 on D.

Set the index of C to 2 on D, move the cursor to sin 70 on S and read 1·9 on D.

Set the index of C to 1 (Index) on D, move the cursor to cos 70 on S and read ·34 on D.

∴ Devn. = +2−4·1+2·3+1·9+0·3

Deviation on 055° C. = +2·4 or 2·4 E.

The important point to watch is the positive and negative signs of the sines and cosines of angles over 90°.

To find the Compass Heading for Maximum Deviation.

Tan Hdg. $= \dfrac{B}{C}$

Example—Given B $= +5$, C $= +3$.

Tan Hdg. $= +\dfrac{5}{3}$

Set the Index of C to 3 on D, move the cursor to 5 on D and read 59° 02′ on T.B.

Tan Hdg.$+$. $\therefore$ Heading $=$ 059 or 239 C.

To find the Compass Heading for Zero Deviation.

Tan Hdg. $= \dfrac{-C}{B}$

Example—

Given B $= -6$, C $= -4$

Tan Hdg. $= \dfrac{-(-4)}{-6} = -\dfrac{4}{6}$

Set the index of C to 6 on D, move the cursor to 4 on D and read 33° 42′ on T.A.

Tan Hdg.—Negative Tangent means second and fourth quadrant.

$\therefore$ Hdg. $= 360 - 33° 42′$ *or* $180 - 33° 42′$.

Heading $= 326° 18′$ *or* $146° 18′$.

Change of Deviation with Change of Magnetic Latitude. Deviation due to Permanent Magnetism varies inversely as H.

I.e. New Devn. : Old Devn. :: Old H : New H.

Set Old H on C1 over Old Devn. on D, then under the New H on C1 read the New Devn. on D.

Example—Coeff. Permanent B (due to force P) was +5, where H was ·24 units. Find Coeff. Permanent B where H is ·18 units.

Set ·24 on C1 over 5 on D, and under ·18 on C1 read 6·66 on D.

New Devn. = +6·66°.

Deviation due to Vertical Soft Iron varies as Tan Dip.

I.e. New Devn. : Old Devn. :: Tan New Dip : Tan Old Dip.

Centre the slide. Move the cursor to the New Dip on T.A. or T.B. and set the Old Dip on T.A. or T.B. to the cursor, then under the Old Devn. on C read the New Devn. on D.

Example—Deviation due to Vertical Soft Iron was +4 where the Dip was 31°. Find the Deviation on the same course where Dip is 60°.

Centre the slide. Move the cursor to 60 on T.B., and set 31 on T.A. to the cursor, then under 4 on C read 11·5 on D.

New Deviation = +11·5°.

$$\text{Tan Dip} = \frac{Z}{H}$$

∴ Deviation varies as $\dfrac{Z}{H}$

I.e. New Devn. = Old Devn. $\times \dfrac{\text{New Z}}{\text{New H}} \times \dfrac{\text{Old H}}{\text{Old Z}}$

Example—Deviation due to Vertical Soft Iron was −3 where H = ·18 units and Z = +·48 units. Find the deviation on the same course where H = ·24 units and Z = −·36 units.

∴ New Devn. = $\dfrac{-3 \times (-·36) \times ·18}{·24 \times ·48}$

Set ·24 on C over 3 on D, move the cursor to ·36 on C, set ·48 on C to the cursor, move the cursor to ·18 on C and read 1·69 on D.

New Devn. $= +1·69$.

Heeling Error Calculations.

$$\text{Coeff. J} = \frac{\text{Heeling Error}}{\text{Angle of Heel} \times \cos \text{co.}}$$

Example—Heeling Error 3°, Angle of Heel 5°, Course 040°.

Set 5 on C over 3 on D, move the cursor to the index of C and set cos 40 on S to the cursor and under the index of C read ·783 on D.

Coeff. J = ·783.

Heeling Error = J . i . cos co.

Where J is the Heeling Error Coefficient, and i is the Angle of Heel.

Example—J = 1·4, i = 6°, Course 038°.

Set the index of C to 1·4 on D, move the cursor to 6 on C, set the index of C to the cursor and under cos 38° on S read 6·6 on D.

Heeling Error = 6·6°.

Gyro Calculations.

Drift in Azimuth with Axis Horizontal.

Drift = 15° sin Lat per hour.
In N. Lat to the right.   In S. Lat to the left.

Example—Find the drift of the Gyro in Lat 47° 20′ N.

Set the index of C to 15 on D, move the cursor to sin 47° 20′ on S and read 11 on D.

Drift = 11° to the Right.

H

Tilt of Gyro Axis.

Tilt = 15′ sin Azimuth.   Cos Lat per minute.

Example—To find the rate of tilt of a gyro in Lat 42° 30′ N., Azimuth 065°.

Set the index of C to 15 on D, move the cursor to sin 65° on S, set the index of C to the cursor, move the cursor to cos 42° 30′ on S and read 10 on D.

Rate of Tilt = 10′ per minute.

Transport Wander.

$$\text{Transport wander} = \frac{G/S \times \sin \text{Track}}{60} \times \tan \text{Lat}.$$

Example—To find the transport wander on Track 040 (T) at G/S 450 knots in Lat 52 N.

Set 60 on C to 450 on D, move the cursor to sin 40 on S, set the index of C to the cursor, move the cursor to tan 52 on TB and read 6·2 on D.

Transport Wander = 6·2°/hour.

Course and Speed Error of the Gyro.

$$\text{Error in degrees} = \frac{\text{Speed in knots} \times \cos \text{co}}{5\pi \cos \text{Lat}}$$

Example—Speed 17 knots. Course 035° T., Lat 48° N.

Set π on C to the index of D, move the cursor to 17 on C, set 5 on C to the cursor, move the cursor to cos 35 on S, set cos 48 on S to the cursor, and under the index of C read 1·33 on D.

Error = 1·33° or 1° 20′.

Distance off by Angle of Depression.

Using Bubble Sextant.

Distance = Height of Eye. Cot Angle of Depression.

Move the cursor to the Height of Eye on C and set the Angle of Depression on T.A. or S.T., as appropriate to the cursor. Then under the index of C read the distance on D.

Example—An aircraft flying at 1500 ft., observed the Angle of Depression of a Light Ship to be 1° 48'.

Set the cursor to 1500 on D and set 1° 48' on S.T. to the cursor. Then under the index of C read 47,750 on D. Move the cursor to the index of C and set 6080 on C to the cursor and under the index of C read 7·85 on D.

Distance = 47,750 ft. = 7·85 nautical miles.

Using a Marine Sextant.

When using a marine sextant the Angle of Depression must be corrected for Dip.

Example—Height of Eye 54 ft. Angle of Depression 7° 40'.

Angle of Depression	7° 40'
Dip for 54 ft.	+ 7·2'
Corrected reading	7° 47·2'

Set the cursor to 54 on D and set 7° 47·2' on T.A. to the cursor, then under the index of C read 395 on D.

Distance 395 ft.

To find the Diameter of the Turning Circle of a Ship.

Turn the Ship through more than 180°, and measure the Angle of Depression of the Wake. Then proceed as above.

Example—Height of Eye 58 ft. Angle of Depression of the Wake, 2° 43′

Angle of Depression	2° 43′
Dip for 58 ft.	+ 7·5′
Corrected reading	2° 50·5′

Set the cursor to 58 on D and set 2° 50·5′ on S.T. to the cursor. Then under the index of C read 1170 on D.

Diameter = 1170 ft.

Revolutions, Pitch and Speed.

To find the Speed for a given Revs. per min.

$$\text{Speed} = \frac{\text{Revs.} \times \text{Pitch} \times 60}{6080}$$

Set the index of C to the Revs. on D, move the cursor to the Pitch on C, set 6080 on C to the cursor, move the cursor to 60 on C and read the speed in knots on D.

Example—91 R.P.M. Pitch 17′ 6″ (= 17·5 ft.)

Set the index of C to 91 on D, move the cursor 17·5 on C, set 6080 on C to the cursor and under 60 on C read 15·7 on D.

Speed 15·7 knots.

To allow for Slip. Say 5 per cent.

Set the index of C, to the Engine Speed on D, and under (100—Slip) on C read the speed on D.

I.e. Set the index of C to 15·7 on D and under ·95 (100—5) on C read 14·9 on D.

Speed corrected for Slip = 14·9 knots.

To find the R.P.M. for a Given Speed.

$$R.P.M. = \frac{Speed \times 6080}{Pitch \times 60}$$

Set the Pitch on C over the Speed on D, move the cursor to 6080 on C, set 60 on C to the cursor and under the index of C read the R.P.M. on D.

Example—Pitch 19 ft. Find the R.P.M. for 18 knots.

Set 19 on C over 18 on D, move the cursor to 6080 on C, set 60 on C to the cursor and under the index of C read 96 on D.

R.P.M. for 18 knots = 96.

To allow for Slip. Say 3 per cent.

Set 97 (100—slip) on C to 96 on D and under the index of C read 989 on D.

R.P.M. allowing for 3 per cent Slip = 98·9.

To find Distance run by Revolutions.

$$Distance = \frac{Revs. \times Pitch}{6080}$$

Set 6080 on C over the Revs. on D, move the cursor to the Pitch on C and read the distance on D.

Example—Pitch 19 ft. 6 in. (19·5 ft.). Engine Revs. 37,400.

H*

Set 6080 on C over 37,400 on D, move the cursor to 19·5 on C and read 119·9 on D.

Distance = 119·9 ml.

To allow for Slip. Say 6 per cent.

Set the Index of C to 119·9 on D and under 94 (100—Slip) on C read 112·7 on D.

Distance allowing for 6 per cent Slip = 112·7 ml.

Speed on the Measured Mile.

$$\text{Speed} = \frac{3600}{\text{Time in seconds}}$$

Set the time in seconds on C over 3600 on D and under the Index of C read the speed on D.

Example—A vessel covered the measured mile in 3 min. 20 sec. (200 sec.).

Set 200 on C over 3600 on D and under the index of C read 18 on D.

Speed 18 knots.

Speed over a Measured Distance.

$$\text{Speed} = \frac{\text{Distance in feet} \times 3600}{\text{Time in seconds} \times 6080} \text{ knots.}$$

Example—A vessel covers a Measured Distance of 7750 ft. in 5 min. 32 sec. (332 sec.).

Set 332 on C over 7750 on D, move the cursor to 3600 on C, set 6080 on C to the cursor and under the index of C read 13·82 on D.

Speed 13·82 knots.

Ships Fuel Consumption Calculations.

The standard formula for these problems may be written:

$$cS^2D = Cs^2d.$$

Where c, s, and d are the original figures for consumption, speed and distance, and C, S, and D the new figures.

Example—A vessel steaming at 12 knots burns 395 tons of fuel to cover a certain distance. How much will she burn to cover the same distance at 14 knots.

In this the distances are the same. d = D.

$$\therefore cS^2 = Cs^2$$
$$or \quad \frac{C}{c} = \frac{S^2}{s^2}$$

Set 12 on C over 14 on D, then over 395 on B read 537 on A.

Consumption 537 tons.

Example—A vessel steaming at 16 knots covers 2150 miles on 590 tons of fuel. How much fuel would she require to cover 2500 miles at 13 knots?

$$cS^2D = Cs^2d$$
$$\therefore C = \frac{cS^2D}{s^2d} = \frac{590 \times 13^2 \times 2500}{16^2 \times 2150}$$

Set 16 on C over 13 on D, move the cursor to 590 on B, set 2150 on B to the cursor, move the cursor to 2500 on B and read 452 on A.

Consumption = 452 tons.

Example—A vessel steaming at 17 knots covers 1800

miles on 640 tons of fuel. At what speed must she steam
to cover 1450 miles on 430 tons of fuel?

$$cS^2D = Cs^2d$$
$$\therefore S^2 = \frac{Cs^2d}{cD}$$

and $S = \sqrt{\dfrac{Cs^2d}{cD}} = \dfrac{\overline{430 \times 17^2 \times 1800}}{640 \times 1450}$

Set 640 on B to 430 on A, move the cursor to 1800
on B, set 1450 on B to the cursor, and under 17 on C
read 15·5 on D.

> Speed 15·5 knots.

Over a given period of time $d = s \times t$ *or* $D = S \times t$
$\therefore cS^2D = Cs^2d$ becomes $cS^2 \times S \times t = Cs^2 \times s \times t$
or $cS^3 = Cs^3$.

Example—A vessel burns 52 tons of fuel a day at
14 knots. What would she burn at 16 knots?
$cS^3 = Cs^3$.

Using the K Scale.

Set the cursor to 14 on D and read 2740 on K.

Set the cursor to 16 on D and read 4100 on K.

Set 2740 on C over 4100 on D and under 52 on C read
77·7 on D.

> Consumption 77·7 tons per day.

Alternative Setting—

$cS^3 = Cs^3$, may be written as $cS^2 \times S = Cs^2 \times s$.

Set 14 on C over 16 on D, move the cursor to 16 on B,
set 14 on B to the cursor and over 52 on B read 77·7
on A.

> Consumption 77·7 tons per day.

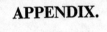

APPENDIX.

APPENDIX I

Gauge Points.

These are special settings, included here, in addition to those specially inscribed on the rule, for the conversion of units. Many of these are also given in the form of Conversion factors. When using the factors, it is a case of simple multiplication, but the factor may be an awkward one to use on a slide rule, as, for instance, centimetres to inches. Here the factor is ·3937. But the same result may be obtained by using the Gauge Points given:

$$cm.: In.: : 66 : 26$$

Set 66 on C (or CF) to 26 on D (or DF). The against any number of centimetres on C (or CF) read the equivalent in inches on D (or DF). And against any number of inches on D (or DF) read the equivalent in centimetres on C (or CF).

For example against 5 on C is found 1·97 on D.

$$5 \text{ cm.} = 1·97 \text{ in.}$$

GAUGE POINTS

Distances and Speeds

Nautical miles	: Statute miles	66 :	76
Nautical miles	: Kilometres	41 :	76
Statute miles	: Kilometres	41 :	66
Yards	: Metres	82 :	75
Feet	: Metres	82 :	25
Inches	: Centimetres	26 :	66
Feet per second	: Miles per hour	44 :	30
Feet per second	: Knots	304 :	180
Metres per second	: Miles per hour	80 :	179
Metres per second	: Knots	34 :	66
Fathoms	: Metres	41 :	75

Areas

Square inches	: Square centimetes	31 : 200
Square feet	: Square metres	140 : 13
Square yards	: Square metres	61 : 51
Acres	: Hectares	42 : 17
Square miles	: Square kilometres	22 : 57

Cubes

Cubic inches	: Cubic centimetres	5 : 82
Cubic feet	: Cubic metres	600 : 17
Cubic yards	: Cubic metres	85 : 65
Cubic metres	: Tons at 40 cu. ft.	17 : 15
Cubic metres	: Tons at 100 cu. ft.	17 : 6

Weights

Ounces	: Grammes	6 : 170
Pounds	: Kilograms	75 : 34
Imperial tons	: Metric tonnes	62 : 63
Grains	: Grammes	108 : 7
Fresh water	: Salt water	38 : 39
Cu. ft. of fresh water	: Pounds	5 : 312

Capacities

Imperial gallons	: U.S. gallons	5 : 6
Imperial gallons	: Litres	55 : 250
Imperial gallons	: Cubic feet	430 : 69
U.S. gallons	: Litres	14 : 53
U.S. gallons	: Cubic feet	800 : 107
Litres	: Cubic feet	170 : 6
Litres	: Pints	25 : 44

Pressures

Inches of mercury	: Feet of water	15 : 17
Inches of mercury	: Pounds per sq. in.	57 : 28
Inches of mercury	: Millibars	22 : 745
Inches of mercury	: Millimetres of mercury	26 : 660

Millimetres of mercury	:	Millibars	45 : 60
Feet of fresh water	:	Pounds per sq. in.	60 : 26
Feet of fresh water	:	Tons per sq. ft.	600 : 167
Pounds per sq. in.	:	Kilograms per sq. cm.	640 : 45

Conversion Factors

To Convert	To	Multiply by
Centimetres	Inches	·3957
Inches	Centimetres	2·540
Metres	Feet	3·281
Feet	Metres	·3048
Kilometres	Statute miles	·6212
Statute miles	Kilometres	1·609
Nautical miles	Kilometres	1·855
Kilometres	Nautical miles	·5389
Nautical miles	Statute miles	1·151
Statute miles	Nautical miles	·868
Imperial gallons	U.S. gallons	1·205
U.S. gallons	Imperial gallons	·8299
Litres	Imperial gallons	·2200
Imperial gallons	Litres	4·546
U.S. gallons	Litres	3·773
Litres	U.S. gallons	·2651
Pints	Litres	·5647
Litres	Pints	1·760
Pounds	Kilograms	·4540
Kilograms	Pounds	2·205
Millibars	Inches of mercury	·02953
Inches of mercury	Millibars	33·86
Feet of salt water	Tons per sq. ft.	·02859
Feet of fresh water	Tons per sq. ft.	·02790
Metres	Yards	1·0936
Yards	Metres	·9144

Conversion Tables

Pence as Decimals of a Shilling Inches as Decimals of a Foot					16ths as Decimals	
Pence or In.	0	$\frac{1}{4}$	$\frac{1}{2}$	$\frac{3}{4}$	1/16	·0625
					2/16	·125
					3/16	·1875
0	·000	.021	·042	·063	4/16	·25
1	·083	·104	·125	·146	5/16	·3125
2	·167	·188	·208	·229	6/16	·375
3	·250	·270	·291	·312	7/16	·4357
4	·333	·354	·375	·395	8/16	·5
5	·416	·437	·458	·478	9/16	·5625
6	·500	·520	·541	·562	10/16	·625
7	·583	·604	·625	·645	11/16	·6875
8	·667	·687	·708	·729	12/16	·75
9	·750	·770	·791	·812	13/16	·8125
10	·833	·854	·875	·895	14/16	·875
11	·917	·937	·958	·979	15/16	·9375

Hours and Minutes as Decimals of a Day

Hrs.	Minutes				Hrs.	Minutes			
	0	15	30	45		0	15	30	45
0	·000	·010	·021	·031	12	·500	·510	·521	·531
1	·042	·052	·063	·073	13	·542	·552	·563	·573
2	·083	·094	·104	·114	14	·583	·594	·604	·614
3	·125	·136	·146	·156	15	·625	·636	·646	·656
4	·167	·177	·188	·198	16	·667	·677	·688	·698
5	·208	·219	·229	·240	17	·708	·719	·729	·740
6	·250	·260	·271	·281	18	·750	·760	·771	·781
7	·292	·302	·312	·323	19	·792	·802	·812	·823
8	·333	·344	·354	·365	20	·833	·844	·854	·865
9	·375	·385	·396	·406	21	·875	·885	·896	·906
10	·417	·427	·438	·448	22	·917	·927	·938	·948
11	·458	·469	·479	·490	23	·958	·969	·979	·990

APPENDIX II

Useful Formulae

$\pi = 3\cdot1416$

Area of a triangle	$= \sqrt{S(S-a)\,(S-b)\,(S-C)}$
where S	$= \frac{1}{2}(a+b+c)$
Area of a triangle	$= \frac{1}{2}$ base $\times$ height
Area of a parallelogram	$=$ length $\times$ height
Area of a trapezoid	$=$ height $\times \frac{1}{2}$ sum of the two parallel sides
Area of a circle	$= \pi r^2 = \dfrac{\pi D^2}{4}$
Circumference of a circle	$= \pi D = 2\,\pi r$
Volume of a cylinder	$= \pi r^2 l = \dfrac{\pi D^2 l}{4}$
Surface area of a cylinder	$= \pi D l +$ area of ends
Volume of sphere	$= \dfrac{\pi D^3}{6} = \dfrac{4\pi r^3}{3}$
Surface area of a sphere	$= \pi D^2$
Volume of a cone	$= \dfrac{1}{3} \times \dfrac{\pi D^2 l}{4} = \dfrac{\pi D^2 l}{12} = \dfrac{\pi r^2 l}{3}$
Surface area of a cone	$= \frac{1}{2}\,\pi D h +$ area of base
where h	$=$ Slant height
Area of Wetted Surface	$= L(1\cdot7D + \text{Coeff} \times B)$

Plane Trigonometry

Sine Formula $\quad \dfrac{a}{\sin A} = \dfrac{b}{\sin B} = \dfrac{c}{\sin C}$

Tangent Formula $\quad \tan\dfrac{A+B}{2} = \dfrac{a-b}{a+b} \times \tan\dfrac{C}{2}$

Haversine Formula hav $A = \dfrac{(s-b)\,(s-c)}{bc}$

where $s = \frac{1}{2}(a+b+c)$

Right-Angled Spherical

Sin Mid Part = Tan Adjacents.
$\qquad$ = Cos Opposites.

Oblique Spherical

Sine Formula $\dfrac{\sin a}{\sin A} = \dfrac{\sin b}{\sin B} = \dfrac{\sin c}{\sin C}$

Cosine Formula $\cos a = \cos b \,.\, \cos c \,.\, +\sin b \,.\, \sin c \,.\, \cos A.$

Tangent Formula $\tan \dfrac{A+B}{2} = \dfrac{\cos \frac{1}{2}(a-b)}{\cos \frac{1}{2}(a+b)} \cot \dfrac{C}{2}$
(for Angles)

$\qquad \operatorname{Tan} \dfrac{A-B}{2} = \dfrac{\sin \frac{1}{2}(a-b)}{\sin \frac{1}{2}(a+b)} \cot \dfrac{C}{2}$

Haversine Formula hav $a = $ hav . A sin b sin c $+$hav (b$\sim$c)
Hav A $= $ [hav a$-$hav (b$\sim$c)] cosec b cosec c

Tangent Formula $\tan \frac{1}{2}(a+b) = \dfrac{\cos \frac{1}{2}(A-B)}{\cos \frac{1}{2}(A+B)} \tan \dfrac{c}{2}$
(for sides)

$\qquad \operatorname{Tan} \frac{1}{2}(a-b) = \dfrac{\sin \frac{1}{2}(A-B)}{\sin \frac{1}{2}(A+B)} \tan \dfrac{c}{2}$

Four-Part Formula. $\quad$ (Cos (I.S.)$-$cos (I.A.) = sin (I.S.)
$\qquad\qquad\qquad\qquad$ cot (O.S.)$-$sin (I.A.) cot (O.A.))

$\quad$ I = Inner, $\qquad$ O = Outer, $\qquad$ S = Side, $\qquad$ A = Angle.

Plane Sailing

D. Lat.	= Dist. Cos Course	= Dep. Cot. Course
Dep.	= Dist. Sin Course	= D. Lat. Tan Course
Dep.	= D. Long. Cos Mid. Lat.	
D. Long.	= Dep. Sec. Mid. Lat.	
Distance	= D. Lat. Sec Course.	= Dep. Cosec Course

$\operatorname{Tan} Co = \dfrac{Dep.}{D.\ Lat.} \quad \operatorname{Sin} Co = \dfrac{Dep.}{Dist.} \quad \operatorname{Cos} Co = \dfrac{D.\ Lat.}{Dist.}$

Mercator Sailing

$$\text{Tan Co} = \frac{\text{D. Long.}}{\text{D.M.P.}} \qquad \text{Dist.} = \text{D. Lat. Sec Co.}$$

Distance by Vertical Angle

$$\theta = \frac{h(\text{ft.}) \times \cdot 565}{d(\text{nm.})}$$

$$d = \frac{h \times \cdot 565}{\theta'}$$

Amplitudes

Sin (Bearing) Amp. = Sin Dec. Sec Lat.
Sin (Time) Amp. = Tan Dec. Tan Lat.

Observations on the Prime Vertical

Sin. Altitude = Sin Dec. Cosec Lat.
Cos. Hour Angle **Q**= Cot Lat. Tan Dec.

Miscellaneous

Sin Azimuth = Sin H.A. Cos Dec. Sec Alt.
Cos Altitude = Sin H.A. Cos Dec. Cosec Azimuth.
Ch. of Alt./Min. = 15' Sin Az. Cos Lat.
Parx. ×in Alt. = Horz. Parx. Cos Alt.
$\frac{1}{2}$ Convergency = $\frac{1}{2}$ D. Long. Sin. Mean Lat.
Distance to Sea Horizon = $1\cdot15 \sqrt{\text{Height.}}$
Dip of the Sea Horizon = $\cdot9984 \sqrt{\text{Height of Eye.}}$

Air Navigation, Flight Planning

$$\text{G.P.H.} = \frac{\text{T.A.S.}}{\text{A.M.P.G.}} = \frac{\text{G./S.}}{\text{G.M.P.G.}}$$

$$\text{A.M.P.G.} = \frac{\text{T.A.S.}}{\text{G.P.H.}}$$

$$\text{G.M.P.H.} = \frac{\text{G./S.}}{\text{G.P.H.}}$$

Distance to Critical Point $= \dfrac{\text{Total Dist.} \times \text{G./S. Home}}{\text{G./S. Out} + \text{G./S. Home}}$

Distance to P.N.R.[2] $= \dfrac{\text{Endurance} \times \text{G./S. Out} \times \text{G./S. Home}}{\text{G./S. Out} + \text{G./S. Home}}$

Time to P.N.R. $= \dfrac{\text{Endurance} \times \text{G.S. Home}}{\text{G./S. Out} + \text{G./S. Home}}$

With Variable Fuel Flow

Distance to P.N.R. $= \dfrac{\text{Fuel Available}}{\dfrac{\text{Fuel Flow}}{\text{G./S.}} \text{out} + \dfrac{\text{Fuel Flow}}{\text{G./S.}} \text{home}}$

Single Heading Flight

$\text{Zn} = \dfrac{21 \cdot 47 \, (H_i - H_o)}{\text{T.A.S.} \sin \theta}$

$\text{Vn} = \dfrac{21 \cdot 47 \, (H_i - H_o)}{A \cdot \sin \theta}$

$\text{Sin Drift} = \dfrac{21 \cdot 47 \, (H_i - H_o)}{A \cdot \sin \theta \times \text{Distance}}$

Meteorology

Change of Height per Mb.

$H(\text{feet}) = \dfrac{96 \cdot T}{P}, \quad H(\text{metres}) = \dfrac{29 \cdot 27 \, T}{P}$

Pressure/Height Formula.

$H_i - H_o (\text{feet}) = 221 \cdot 1 \, T \, (\text{Log} \, P_o - \text{Log} \, P_i)$
$H_i - H_o (\text{metres}) = 67 \cdot 4 \, T \, (\text{Log} \, P_o - \text{Log} \, P_i)$

Adiabatic Temperature Change.

$\text{Log} \, T_i - \text{Log} \, T_o = 0 \cdot 288 \, (\text{Log} \, p_i - \text{Log} \, p_o)$

Geostrophic Wind Equation.

$V = \dfrac{\dfrac{dp}{ds}}{2 \omega \rho \sin \theta}$

Gradient Wind Equation.

$$V = \frac{\dfrac{dp}{ds}}{2\omega\rho\sin\theta} \pm \frac{V^2}{2\,r\omega\sin\theta}$$

Gyro Formula

Drift in Azimuth $= 15°$ sin Lat/hour.
Rate of Tilt $= 15'$ sin Az. cos Lat/Minute.
Transport Wander $= \dfrac{G./S.\ \sin Tr.}{60} \times \tan$ Lat.

Course and Speed Error.

Error in degrees $= \dfrac{\text{Speed in knots . cos Co.}}{5\pi . \cos \text{Lat.}}$

Compass Formulae.

Devn$=$
$\quad A+B$. sin Co$+C$. cos Co$+D$. sin 2 Co$+E$. cos 2 Co.

Maximum Deviation.

Tan Hdg. $= \dfrac{B}{C}$

Zero Deviation.

Tan Hdg. $= \dfrac{-C}{B}$

Change of Deviation with Change of Mag. Lat.

Deviation due to Hard Iron.

New Devn $= \dfrac{\text{Old Devn} \times \text{Old H}}{\text{New H}}$

Deviation due to Vertical Soft Iron.

New Devn $= \dfrac{\text{Old Devn} \times \tan \text{New Dip}}{\text{Tan Old Dip}}$

$\qquad\qquad = \text{Old Devn} \times \dfrac{\text{Old H}}{\text{New H}} \times \dfrac{\text{New Z}}{\text{Old Z}}$

Coeff J $= \dfrac{\text{Heeling Error}}{\text{Angle of Heel . cos Co.}}$

Heeling Error.

Heeling Error $= J . i . \cos C_o.$

Slewing Spheres.

$\text{Tan } 2M = \dfrac{E}{D}$

APPENDIX III

Approximate Weight per Cubic Foot of Various Metals

	lbs.		lbs.
Wrought iron – –	480	Aluminium – –	167
Cast iron – – –	450	Gun-metal – –	531
Cast steel – – –	490	Gold – –	1204
Copper – – –	550	Mercury – –	849
Brass – – –	525	Platinum – –	1344
Lead – – –	710	Silver – –	654
Tin – – –	462	Antimony – –	420
Zinc – – –	449	Bronze – –	513
White metal – –	456	Nickel – –	560

Approximate Weight per Cubic Foot of Various Woods

	lbs.		lbs.
Ash – – –	47	Junglewood – –	57
Beech – – –	45	Lignum Vitae – –	83
Birch – – –	45	Lime – – –	35
Boxwood – – –	61	Mahogany, Honduras	35
Cedar, American –	35	,, Spanish	53
,, Lebanon –	30	Maple – –	42
,, W. Indies –	47	Oak, African – –	62
Chestnut – – –	38	,, American –	50
Cork – – –	15	,, English –	52
Cottonwood, Green	46	Pine, Red – –	34
,, Dry –	24	,, Norway –	34
Cypress – – –	27	,, Pitch –	38
Deal, Norway –	43	,, White –	29
,, U.K. –	30	,, Yellow –	32
Ebony – – –	74	Redwood, Green –	60
Elm, Canadian –	45	,, Dry –	27
,, English –	35	Sycamore – –	37
Fir, Douglas –	38	Teak, Africa – –	60
,, Spruce –	34	,, Burma –	54
Larch – –	34	,, India –	46
Greenheart – –	71	,, Philippine –	48
Hornbeam – –	47	Yew – – –	50
Ironwood – –	71		

Approximate S.G. of Various Oils

Aniseed	–	–	1·00	Palm	–	–	0·91
Castor	–	–	0·97	Paraffin	–	–	0·91
Coconut	–	–	0·93	Petrol	–	–	0·76
Colza	–	–	0·92	Petroleum, crude		–	0·85
Cottonseed	–	–	0·93	Pine	–	–	0·85
Linseed	–	–	0·94	Poppyseed	–	–	0·92
Neatsfoot	–	–	0·92	Rapeseed	–	–	0·91
Kerosene	–	–	0·80	Soya Bean	–	–	0·92
Olive	–	–	0·92	Turpentine	–	–	0·87
China Wood	–	–	0·94	Seal	–	–	0·93
Lardine	–	–	0·97	Sperm	–	–	0·88
Nigerseed	–	–	0·93	Tallow oil	–	–	0·91
Palm Nut	–	–	0·95	Whale	–	–	0·93

Approximate Space required to Stow 1 Ton of Various Grains and Seeds

			cu. ft.				cu. ft.
Aniseed	–	–	120	Mustard	–	–	60
Barley	–	–	60	Negro corn	–	–	53
Bushwheat	–	–	66	Niger	–	–	64
Caraway	–	–	62	Oats, clipped	–	–	74
Castor	–	–	72	,, unclipped	–	–	83
Cloves	–	–	48	Onion	–	–	65
Coriander	–	–	130	Paddy	–	–	65
Corn	–	–	54	Peas	–	–	50
Cotton	–	–	75	Poppy	–	–	71
Croton	–	–	80	Rapeseed	–	–	60
Fennel	–	–	95	Rice	–	–	52
Flax	–	–	57	Rye	–	–	55
Guinea maize	–	–	80	Sesame	–	–	60
Hemp	–	–	68	Soya beans	–	–	55
Kernels	–	–	48	Spinach	–	–	70
Linseed	–	–	58	Sugar beet	–	–	135
Locust beans	–	–	78	Sunflower	–	–	105
Maize	–	–	54	Vetch	–	–	50
Millet	–	–	50	Turkish millet	–	–	53
Mirobolans	–	–	70	Wheat	–	–	52

The figures given are for cargo in bags. For bulk cargo decrease these figures by about 10 per cent.

APPENDIX IV

Weights and Measures

LINEAR MEASURE

12 inches	= 1 foot	5280 feet	= 1 statute mile
3 feet	= 1 yard	6080 feet	= 1 nautical mile
5½ yards	= 1 rod or pole	1760 yards	= 1 statute mile
40 poles	= 1 furlong	608 feet	= 1 cable
220 yards	= 1 furlong	10 cables	= 1 nautical mile
8 furlongs	= 1 statute mile		
100 links	= 1 chain	6 feet	= 1 fathom
22 yards	= 1 chain		
10 chains	= 1 furlong		

SQUARE MEASURE

144 sq. ins.	= 1 sq. foot
9 sq. feet	= 1 sq. yard
30¼ sq. yards	= 1 sq. rod, sq. pole or perch
40 perches	= 1 rood
40 roods	= 1 acre
4840 sq. yds.	= 1 acre
640 acres	= 1 sq. mile

CUBIC MEASURE

1728 cu. ins.	= 1 cu. ft.
27 cu. ft.	= 1 cu. yd.
40 cu. ft.	= 1 ton (cargo)
100 cu. ft.	= 1 ton register
35 cu. ft.	= 1 ton displacement

AVOIRDUPOIS

16 drams	= 1 ounce	20 cwts.	= 1 ton
16 ounces	= 1 pound	2240 pounds	= 1 ton
14 pounds	= 1 stone	100 pounds	= 1 cwt. (American)
28 pounds	= 1 quarter	2000 pounds	= 1 ton (American)
4 quarters	= 1 cwt.		

LIQUID MEASURE

4 gills	= 1 pint	36 gallons	= 1 barrel
2 pints	= 1 quart	54 gallons	= 1 hogshead
4 quarts	= 1 gallon	72 gallons	= 1 puncheon

CORN MEASURE

2 pints	= 1 quart	4 pecks	= 1 bushel
4 quarts	= 1 gallon	8 bushels	= 1 quarter
2 gallons	= 1 peck	5 quarters	= 1 load

Metric System

LENGTH

10 Millimetres	=1 centimetre	10 Metres	=1 dekametre
10 Centimetres	=1 decimetre	10 Dekametres	=1 hectometre
10 Decimetres	=1 metre	10 Hectometres	=1 kilometre

CAPACITY

10 Centilitres	=1 decilitre	10 Dekalitres	=1 hectolitre
10 Decilitres	=1 litre	10 Hectolitres	=1 kilolitre
10 Litres	=1 dekalitre		

MASS

10 Milligrams	=1 decigram	10 Hectograms	=1 kilogram
10 Decigrams	=1 centigram	10 Kilograms	=1 myriagram
10 Centigrams	=1 gram	10 Myriagrams	=1 quintal
10 Grams	=1 dekagram	10 Quintals	=1 tonne
10 Dekagrams	=1 hectogram